ISBN 978-1-5284-8293-6
PIBN 10139606

WISDOM AND WIT.

BURNS AND OATES, PRINTERS, LONDON.

THE WISDOM AND WIT

OF

LESSED THOMAS MORE

BEING EXTRACTS FROM SUCH OF HIS WORKS AS
WERE WRITTEN IN ENGLISH

COLLECTED AND EDITED

BY

REV. T. E. BRIDGETT, C.S.S.R.

AUTHOR OF "LIFE OF BLESSED THOMAS MORE," ETC.

Well furnyshed of one speciall thynge, without which all lernynge is halfe lame.
What is that? quod he. Mary, quod I, a good mother wyt.—Sir T. More,
Dialogue, p. 153

LONDON: BURNS & OATES, Ld.
NEW YORK: CATHOLIC PUBLICATION SOCIETY CO.
1892

PREFACE.

IN 1891 I published the *Life and Writings of Sir Thomas More*. In that volume I gave a short account of his various books and pamphlets both in Latin and English, together with numerous extracts and translations. Several of my reviewers expressed a hope that a complete Library Edition of the Works of More might soon be undertaken. Perhaps the present collection may serve as a sample both of his matter and manner, and hasten the desired reprint. As such a publication, however, would be very costly, and must of course retain the old spelling, it would not bring the wisdom or the wit of the great writer much nearer to the general public, and the selection I have made would still be useful. I had announced a reprint, somewhat abridged, of the holy martyr's *Dialogue of Comfort against Tribulation*, written by him in the Tower; but I am glad to find there is a remainder of Dolman's reprint still on sale by Mr. Baker, of 1 Soho Square. I have, therefore, merely added extracts from it to selections from his other writings. I have thought it better not to reproduce here any of the passages of More's various writings that I have interwoven into his life. Thus the two

books supplement each other. While I have moder-
nised the spelling I have not ventured to make any
change in words or structure. A very few verbal
explanations in the notes will remove any difficulty
that could be experienced from archaic language.
More's style is easy compared with that of many later
writers.

A volume of Extracts from Sir Thomas More's
writings was printed at Baltimore in 1841 by the Rev.
Joseph Walter, an American Catholic priest, author
of a Life of More.[1] I have made my own collection
independently.

The compilers of our great philological dictionaries
are at length giving to Sir Thomas More's writings
the attention they deserve. They would well repay
a careful search by students of our language. To
facilitate such search I have given careful references to
the page of the folio edition, and where attention is
specially drawn to phraseology, as in Part V., even to
the marginal letter of each page. Copies of the
original editions of More's writings are excessively
rare. Even the British Museum has only a very few.
I have used throughout the great collection of his
English works, made by his nephew William Rastell,
and printed by John Cawood, John Waly, and
Richard Tottell in 1557. It is printed in the old
black-letter type, and contains 1458 pages in double

---

[1] Both works were reprinted in England by *Dolman*, and are long
out of print.

columns. The Antwerp reprint of the *Dialogue of Comfort*, made by John Fowler in 1573, professes to be corrected by collation " of sundry copies " in MS. But I have found that, wherever it differs from Rastell's edition, the latter has intrinsic evidence of giving the correct reading. The fact that it was thrice printed on the Continent—in 1573, 1574, and 1578—is a great proof that this treatise was indeed a " comfort against tribulation " to the persecuted Catholics of England or their countrymen in exile. The modern reader will find that it has lost nothing of its charm or of its utility.

I have ventured to prefix to my selection a short essay on the wisdom and wit of Blessed More.

T. E. Bridgett, C.SS.R.

ENGLISH WORKS OF MORE.

Various Youthful Poems.

Life of John Picus, Earl of Mirandula (a translation).

History of King Richard III. (written in 1513).

Four Last Things (written 1522).

Dialogue Concerning Heresies (1528, quoted as " *Dialogue* ").

Supplication of Souls (1529).

Confutation of Tindale (1532).

Answer to Frith (1533).

Apology (1533).

*Debellation of Salem and Bizance (1533).

Answer to the Masker (1533).

*Dialogue of Comfort against Tribulation (1534).

Treatise on the Passion (1535).

Letters.

CONTENTS.

INTRODUCTORY ESSAY

ON

THE WISDOM AND WIT OF BLESSED THOMAS.[1]

I. HIS WISDOM.

By wisdom, we may understand a true and deep knowledge of the nature of human life, the purpose for which it has been given, and the means by which that purpose may be best attained. By wisdom, we understand also the penetration of the truths of faith, the power of comparing spiritual things with spiritual, as also with things natural, and of making human literature and philosophy the cheerful handmaids of Divine revelation. Of Blessed Thomas More's theoretical wisdom, the extracts given in the present volume, though suffering much from being separated from their context, will give, at least, a glimpse. But wisdom is above all things practical. He, indeed, cannot be said to possess it who is not possessed by it and guided by it. Without attempting a biography of More, I may glance here at the wisdom which dignified and sanctified his life. The general outlines of that life I may suppose in the memory of my reader.

[1] The substance of the following essay is from two lectures delivered by the author, in Chelsea, in 1890 and 1891.

I   (1)

When More was a youth in his father's house, he conceived the design of nine pageants, or emblems, to be executed either in painting or tapestry, for which he composed, in English and Latin verses, the mottoes or explanations. These pageants represented the life of man, not exactly in the seven stages which Shakespeare has made so famous, but through the whole range of time and eternity. They represented Childhood, Youth, Love, Age, Death, Fame, Time, and Eternity ; and, lastly, the Poet summing up the whole. Death, of course, boasts that he has conquered all. Then Fame steps in :—

> O cruel *Death*, thy power I confound ;
> When thou a noble man hast brought to ground
> Maugre thy teeth, to live cause him shall I
> Of people in perpetual memory—

words which are strikingly fulfilled in the case of the young writer, whose fame will never perish on this earth. In the seventh pageant Time scoffs at the promises of Fame, since Time in its progress will destroy the world itself, and then Fame will be mute. Eternity rebukes Time, which is but the revolution of the sun and moon ; true goods and true fame shall subsist throughout eternity, when time itself is dead. The poet then concludes that nothing is of value but the love of the Eternal God, and nothing worth hoping for but His possession. We do not generally attach much importance to the sentiments expressed in poetry by a clever youth as regards religion or philosophy, for he easily appropriates whatever he finds at hand, and he may write a theme on the brevity of life or the vanity of fortune, without being the less eager to have a long life and plenty of its good things. But the life of Blessed Thomas

More shows that from his boyhood he had thoroughly imbibed the philosophy of time and eternity which he thus expressed. It would be an interesting task for the artist and the poet to picture his beautiful life and death, his fame and his eternal recompense, in a series of pageants. I can only attempt this very faintly.

And first as regards his *Early Manhood*. In the second of his pageants More makes his young man say :—

> To hunt and hawk, to nourish up and feed
> The greyhound to the course, the hawk to the flight,
> And to bestride a good and lusty steed,
> These things become a very man indeed.

But in none of these things did More make the delight and the glory of his own youth to consist. That he preferred Latin and Greek to hunting and hawking might betoken only a difference of taste, not moral or spiritual excellence. His biographers, however, tell us that, amid his first literary triumphs, in his first success as a lawyer and a politician, the thought of the emptiness of this world took so deep a hold on his soul that he spent four years in the practice of devotion and extraordinary austerity among the Carthusians, debating whether he should either retire altogether from the world's cares and pleasures, or, as a priest, in an austere and active order, labour for the world's improvement. He wrote the life and translated some of the spiritual works of Pico della Mirandola, a young Italian nobleman of marvellous talent, and no less holiness, who had abandoned his great possessions, and resolved, " fencing himself with the crucifix, barefoot walking about the world, in every town and castle to preach Christ," and who was about to enter the Dominican Order for this

purpose, when he died at the early age of thirty-two.   More
had clearly taken Pico for his model, though it was not
God's will that he should execute his plans any more than
Pico himself.   In his interior spirit, however, he copied him
closely.   He tells us, among other things, that when the
Count of Mirandola was dying, and some mistaken consolers
were reminding him that his early death would free him
from many pains and sorrows which a longer life would
certainly bring, the dying man said, with a smile : " No,
no, that is not the advantage of death.   It is that it puts
an end to sin, and to the danger of offending and losing
God."   To keep himself unspotted by the world, and to be
found at death spotless in the presence of his God, was the
wisdom and philosophy of Blessed More as well as of
Pico.

Another pageant !   When More, for reasons I need not
now enter on, had decided that he should marry and pursue
the legal career to which his father had destined him, he
gave himself heartily to his profession, because it was the
will of God, though he never seems to have regarded it with
any predilection.   He is said to have been the first
Englishman who ever raised himself to distinction by
oratory.   He was a beautiful speaker, and the power of his
mind and his grasp of law were such that he was sure of
success if right was on his side, and he would never
undertake a civil case until he had first assured himself of
this.   He soon came to make as a barrister an income
which, if we take account of the change in the value of
money, would compete with the great incomes of the most
successful pleaders in our own days.   He had become also
a great favourite with the citizens of London, and was sent

to Flanders on an important embassy. What were now the thoughts and feelings of the *Successful Man of the World* ? Was the world become a more substantial reality ? Had heaven faded away into the thin azure ? Far from it. At this time, in the year 1516, when he was thirty-eight years old, he wrote his famous *Utopia*. The citizens of this model republic have but the light of Nature. Though divided in their opinions about religion, there was, says More, one matter in which all were agreed : that death is a boon and not a calamity. In describing the public worship of this imaginary people, he says : "Then they pray that God may give them an easy passage at last to Himself, not presuming to set limits to Him, how early or late it should be ; but, if it may be wished for without derogating from His supreme authority, they desire to be quickly delivered, and to be taken to Himself, though by the most terrible kind of death, rather than to be detained long from seeing Him by the most prosperous course of life ".

In another passage More thus described their views of life, death, and eternity : " Though they are compassionate to all that are sick, yet they lament no man's death, except they see him loath to part with life. They think that such a man's appearance before God cannot be acceptable to Him who being called on does not go out cheerfully, but is backward and unwilling, and is, as it were, dragged to it. They are struck with horror when they see any die in this manner, and carry them out in silence and with sorrow, and praying God that He would be merciful to the errors of the departed soul, they lay the body in the ground ; but when any die cheerfully and full of hope they do not mourn for them, but sing hymns when they carry out their bodies, commending their souls very earnestly to God." Do not say that this is Utopian in the modern sense of the word, that is to say, chimerical or impossible. These were the thoughts and feelings that guided the whole life of Blessed Thomas More. There is, however, a satirical force in them : that men who had but the light of Nature should welcome their appearance before God, while Christians, to whom is promised the Beatific Vision, should shrink from it, defer it as long as possible, and speak with bated breath of the " poor " souls who have gone to enjoy it !

Let me point to another pageant, that of the *Great Statesman*. In his boyish verses Blessed Thomas had described the elderly man :—

> With locks thin and hoar,
> Wise and discreet, the public weal therefore
> He helps to rule.

He himself arrived at this stage, a knight, a privy councillor, the king's secretary, orator on great occasions, treasurer of the exchequer, negotiator of treaties, ambassador to the imperial court, personal attendant on the king in his pomps and splendours. Had all these things dazzled him? Not in the least. In the year 1522, when he was forty-four years old, he sat down to write a book on *The Four Last Things*, that is, Death, Judgment, Heaven and Hell. We see in this book with what thoughts he kept his heart humble. He is but an actor in a gay coat on the stage of life, which he must soon quit. He is a condemned malefactor already in the cart that will carry him to the gallows. The road may be long or short, but the sentence is irrevocably passed, and to the place of execution he must surely come. Some will exclaim that this is a gloomy view of life.

Well, More calls it "homely". It is a true one as regards this world, and enough to make any man sober who entertains it. Yet in the depths of his heart Blessed Thomas was travelling, not to the gallows, but to the door of Paradise, though he could only enter it by death. Erasmus, writing of More at this very time of his public life, says that among his intimate friends he would often speak of the next life in such a way that they knew it was to him the great reality, and that he nourished *optima spes*, the most excellent and assured hope, of its attainment.

Let me here anticipate a difficulty. Do not such views rob human life of all interest and make the heart cold? If a man is thoroughly persuaded that all good is in eternity, surely he will not only desire his own death, but the death of all whom he loves, at least if he thinks them prepared for eternity. I would answer such reasoning not by reasoning, but by experience. Was Blessed Thomas More a gloomy, a cold, or a listless man? Was he incompetent or careless in worldly affairs? He seems to have been raised up for the very purpose of teaching us that true piety and true Christian hope have nothing in common with sadness or imbecility. This man, whose heart was in the next world, was merry and brilliant in his conversation and his writings, a deep student, and an accomplished statesman. As regards his affections and his thoughts about the death of others, let one fact speak. When his favourite daughter, Margaret, was struck down by a terrible disease, and given up by the physicians, at the very point of death, as it seemed, the father went with his riven heart into his oratory, and there prayed so fervently that she might be spared a little longer that, when she quite suddenly recovered, all the bystanders attributed it to the efficacy of his prayers. Some may see inconsistency in this. But we find the same inconsistency in St. Paul. In his Epistle to the Philippians he tells us how " he desired to be dissolved and to be with Christ," and how to him " to live was Christ, but to die was gain ". Yet in the same epistle we find that when a holy disciple of his, the Bishop Epaphroditus, was " sick nigh unto death," St. Paul prayed most earnestly for his recovery, and made others pray, and when Epaphroditus was restored to health the apostle says : " God had mercy upon him, and net on him only, but on me also, lest I should have sorrow upon sorrow ". No, it is not the will of God that we should be heartless, nor is it the will of God that, until His will is re-vealed, we should be indifferent to our loved ones' life or death, nor that even when they have gone to their reward we should be unmoved at our own loss, although we rejoice for their sake. Did not our Divine Lord Himself shed tears over the grave of Lazarus, His beloved Lazarus? Blessed Thomas More told Margaret that had it then pleased God to take her away he had made up his mind to have nothing more to do with public life, but would have given himself entirely to preparation for his own death.

From his childhood he had kept himself in readiness for that call ; he had awaited it in his merry boyhood, in his innocent yet active youth, in his busy and prosperous man-hood. He had meditated on death and eternity in the schools of the university, in his beautiful home, in the tribunals of the law, in the courts of princes : " As the hart panteth after the fountains of water, so my soul panteth after Thee, O God ; my soul hath thirsted after the strong living God ; when, when shall I come and appear before the face of

God?" His life had been a very happy one: he had never sought wealth and honours, yet they had come to him, and in the midst of wealth and honours he had practised true religion, as described by St. James: "Visiting the fatherless and the widows in their affliction and keeping himself unspotted from the world". In one of his early poems on Fortune, taking the well-known image of a woman turning a great wheel to which her clients cling, he had used these words :—

> She suddenly enhanceth them aloft,
> And suddenly mischieveth all the flock ;
> The head that late lay easily and full soft
> Instead of pillows lieth after on the block.

If to Blessed More's angel guardian was then revealed the future death by which his charge should glorify God, he must have bent with loving veneration over that terrible but glorious word—the block. Frequently had More awaited death calmly when multitudes were dying around him of the sweating sickness ; but he was not to die amidst the multitude. For our instruction he was to be our teacher of detachment and Christian hope in the dungeon of the Tower and on the scaffold of Tower Hill. Who has ever read unmoved how, when his writing materials, with which he had composed his beautiful book called *Dialogue of Comfort against Tribulation*, were taken from him, he closed the shutters of his cell, saying, with a smile: " The goods are gone, the shop may be shut," and there remained in prayer and meditation, caring nothing for the light of day because the light of eternity was already flooding his soul ? He never laid himself down to sleep, after the labours of a well-spent day, more calmly than he stretched himself on the scaffold to await the axe of the executioner. But what is it we so much admire in this death? Many a man before and since has met death bravely. Not only in the excitement of a field of battle, or the enthusiasm of a rescue from a fire, but calmly in the execution of duty; as when the captain stands erect upon the sinking ship while he sees the last boat depart with the women and children, sustained by the sense of a duty nobly discharged to the end. All admiration to such deaths! All honour to such men! But it is not mere physical or moral courage we honour in the death of Blessed Thomas More. It is that his death was willing though not wilful. One word of compliance and he would have been carried from the Tower to the palace of the king triumphantly. Little shame would have been his, for all his former associates had yielded. But he could not yield without doing wrong to his conscience and his God, though his fidelity brought his family to penury and cost his own life. But besides this, we honour the death of Blessed Thomas More for special reasons. All the martyrs have accepted death to be faithful to their God, but not all have desired death; at least they have not desired it throughout their life. To him death was the goal of life, to him it was the gate of eternity, to him eternity had been ever the only reality, the only hope that makes life worth living. Pleasure. literary fame, wealth, the smiles of princes, had only proved to him how little, how mean, how worthless are all the goods this life can offer; and his soul thirsted for the strong God from the midst of weakness, for the living God from the midst of death. Such was the wisdom that guided the life of More. We may therefore listen to him with confidence discoursing on such subjects. He carried out consistently what he had written in his early manhood :—

> Why lovest thou so this brittle worldes joy?
> Take all the mirth, take all the phantasies,
> Take every game, take every wanton toy,
> Take every sport that men can thee devise,
> And among them all, on warrantise,
> Thou shalt no pleasure comparable find
> To th' inward gladness of a virtuous mind.
>
> So should the lover of God esteem that he
> Which all the pleasure hath, mirth and disport
> That in this world is possible to be,
> Yet till the time that he may once resort
> Unto that blessed, joyful, heavenly port,
> Where he of God may have the glorious sight,
> Is void of perfect joy and sure delight.[1]

II. HIS WIT.

In the time of Sir Thomas More the words wit and wisdom had almost or altogether the same meaning, yet the quality that we now designate by wit was ever distinct from wisdom, though by no means opposed to it. Wisdom and wit are like heat and light. In addition to knowledge, wit supposes a play of the imagination or the fancy, a faculty of detecting hidden congruities or incongruities, and of bringing images or ideas together in such a way as to cause both surprise and pleasure to the bearer or reader. I take wit here in its generic sense, not as distinct from humour but as comprising it. To defend the use of wit would be as absurd as to defend the human intellect and the cultivation of its

---

[1] Development by More of two of the maxims of Pico della Mirandola.

faculties. To apologise for the union of wit with sanctity
would be as superfluous as to apologise for the use of poetic
imagery, and exalted language by inspired prophets. Yet,
as wit is of various kinds, it may be asked whether there is
not something at least incongruous in employing jokes and
laughter-moving sentences in serious religious controversy,
or in exciting merriment and fun in the midst of spiritual
discourses, and while treating serious or even pathetic
themes. This, nevertheless, is a characteristic of th e genius
of Blessed Thomas More, and it seems to demand, not
so much defence, as explanation, lest it should be mis-
understood.

In More's time, the English prided themselves on being
a merry nation, though Froissart remarks that they took
their mirth sometimes *moult tristement.* But merriment or
mirth as very clearly distinguished from levity or want of
seriousness. No one could condemn levity of character
more severely than did this gay and mirthful, yet most
earnest-minded writer, whose character we are considering.
The following passage will both state his serious view of life,
and serve as a specimen of his bright and witty style of
writing :—

"An evil and a perilous life live they that will in this
world not labour and work, but live either in idleness or in
idle business, driving forth all their days in gaming [1] for
their pastime, as though that else their time could never
pass, but the sun would ever stand even still over their
heads and never draw to night, but if they draw away the
day with dancing or some such other goodly gaming. God

[1] By the context it appears that gaming here means games or amuse-
ments in general.

sent men hither to wake and work ; and as for sleep and gaming (if any gaming be good in this vale of misery, in this time of tears), it must serve but for a refreshing of the weary body; for rest and recreation be but as a sauce, and sauce should (ye wot well) serve for a faint and weak stomach to get it the more appetite to the meat, and not for increase its voluptuous pleasure in every greedy glutton, that hath in himself sauce malapert enough. And therefore, likewise as it were a fond feast that had all the table full of sauce, and so little meat therewith, that the guests should go thence as empty as they came thither ; so is it surely a very mad ordered life that hath but little time bestowed in any fruitful business, and all the substance idly spent in play." [1]

It is clear from these words of Blessed Thomas that if he indulged in any merriment, or defended its use, it had no connection in his mind with that levity and frivolity against which our Divine Master uttered His anathema when He said : " Blessed are they that mourn : woe to you that now laugh ". The blessedness is to those who mourn over sin, the woe to those who laugh at sin or in sin, or who make their whole life a frivolous pastime. It is not a woe pronounced against those who laugh at what is laughable in due season. Laughter is like anger : it may be good or bad, according to circumstances. We must consider both the person who laughs and the object of his laughter. Laughter does not befit the wilful enemies of God, though it may be sometimes skilfully and lawfully awakened in such to lead them to a better mind. Laughter in applause of what is wicked, vile, or impure is criminal laughter. " A fool

[1] *Answer to Masker*, Works, 1047.

will laugh at sin," says the Holy Ghost. Laughter at incongruous trifles which are innocent belongs by right to childhood and youth, yet it may have its season even in the life of the wisest and the saintliest; while laughter at the errors, the vices, the foolish pretences of men, may be a participation in that Divine sarcasm or irony which is attributed to God. "Why have the Gentiles raged and the people desired vain things : the kings of the earth stood up, and the princes met together against the Lord and against His Christ ? He that dwelleth in heaven shall laugh at them, and the Lord shall deride them." The spectacle of worms of earth in revolt against their Creator, of earthly kings contending with the King of heaven, this spectacle is worthy of—which shall I say, laughter or tears ? Of both, according as we regard it. It "makes the angels weep," said our great poet, by a bold figure. It makes God laugh, says the Psalmist, by a still bolder figure.

I do not remember that Blessed Thomas More has anywhere discussed in general the lawfulness or congruity of laughter, or the moral fitness of witty terms of expression in writing on Divine or spiritual things. In his *Dialogue of Comfort against Tribulation* he touches slightly on the subject, and if his tone is apologetical it befitted the modesty of his character, and it must be remembered that he is inquiring, not as to the lawfulness of mirth in general in our human life, but as to the expediency of turning to it for consolation when God is sending afflictions. (In the following dialogue Vincent is a young nobleman, Antony his aged, wise, and holy uncle.)

"*Vincent.*—And first, good Uncle, ere we proceed farther, I will be bold to move you one thing more of that we talked when I was here before. For when I revolved in my mind again the things that were concluded here by you, methought ye would in nowise, that in any tribulation men should seek for comfort either in worldly thing or fleshly, which mind, Uncle, of yours, seemeth somewhat hard. For a merry tale with a friend refresheth a man much, and without any harm lighteneth his ·mind, and amendeth his courage ; so that it seemeth but well done to take such recreation. And Solomon saith, I trow, that men should in heaviness give the sorry man wine to make him forget his sorrow.[1] And St. Thomas saith, that proper pleasant talking, which is called εὐτραπελία,[2] is a good virtue, serving to refresh the mind, and make it quick and lusty to labour and study again, where continual fatigation would make it dull and deadly.

" *Antony*.—Cousin, I forgot not that point, but I longed not much to touch it. For neither might I well utterly forbid it, where the cause might hap to fall that it should not hurt ; and, on the other side, if the case so should fall, methought yet it should little need to give any man counsel to it. Folk are prone enough to such fantasies of their own mind. You may see this by ourselves, which coming now together, to talk of as earnest, sad matter as men can devise, were fallen yet even at the first into wanton, idle tales. And of truth, Cousin, as you know very well, myself am of nature even half a giglot [3] and more. I would I could as easily mend my fault, as I can well know it ; but scant can I refrain it, as old a fool as I am ; howbeit, so partial will I not be to my fault as to praise it.

[1] Proverbs xxxi. 6.   [2] Summa. 2, 2ₐₑ, q. 168, a. 2.
[3] A giddy fellow, always ready to laugh.

"But for that you require my mind in the matter, whether men in tribulation may not lawfully seek recreation and comfort themselves with some honest mirth : first, agreed that our chief comfort must be in God, and that with Him we must begin, and with Him continue, and with Him end also : a man to take now and then some honest worldly mirth, I dare not be so sore as utterly to forbid it, since good men and well learned have in some caseall owed it, specially for the diversity of divers men's minds. For else, if we were all such as would God we were, and such as natural wisdom would we should be, and is not all clean excusable that we be not in deed, I would then put no doubt, but that unto any man the most comfortable talking that could be, were to hear of heaven : whereas now, God help us l our wretchedness is such, that in talking awhile thereof, men wax almost weary, and as though to hear of heaven were a heavy burden, they must refresh themselves after with a foolish tale. Our affection towards heavenly joys waxeth wonderful cold. If dread of hell were as far gone, very few would fear God : but that yet a little sticketh in our stomachs.

"Mark me, Cousin, at the sermon, and commonly to-wards the end, somewhat the preacher speaketh of hell and heaven. Now, while he preacheth of the pains of hell, still they stand yet and give him the hearing ; but as soon as he cometh to the joys of heaven, they be busking them backward and flock-meal fall away. It is in the soul somewhat as it is in the body. Some are there of nature, or of evil custom, come to that point that a worse thing sometimes steadeth them more than a better. Some man, if he be sick, can away with no wholesome meat, nor no medicine can go down with him, but if it be tempered with some such thing for his fantasy, as maketh the meat or the medicine less wholesome than it should be. And yet while it will be no better, we must let him have it so. Cassianus, that very virtuous man, rehearseth in a certain collection of his, that a certain holy father, in making of a sermon, spake of heaven and heavenly things so celestially, that much of his audience with the sweet sound thereof, began to forget all the world, and fall asleep. Which, when the father beheld, he dissembled their sleeping, and suddenly said unto them, I shall tell you a merry tale. At which word, they lifted up their heads and harkened unto that. And after the sleep therewith broken, heard him tell on of heaven again. In what wise that good father rebuked then their untoward minds, so dull unto the thing that all our life we labour for, and so quick and lusty towards other trifles, I neither bear in mind, nor shall here need to rehearse. But thus much of the matter sufficeth for our purpose, that whereas you demand me whether in tribulation men may not sometimes refresh themselves with worldly mirth and recreation, I can no more say ; but he that cannot long endure to hold up his head and hear talking of heaven, except he be now and then between (as though heaven were heaviness) refreshed with a merry, foolish tale, there is none other remedy, but you must let him have it. Better would I wish it, but I cannot help it.

"Howbeit, let us by mine advice at the leastwise make those kinds of recreation as short and as seldom as we can. Let them serve us but for sauce, and make them not our meat : and let us pray unto God, and all our good friends for us, that we may feel such a savour in the delight of heaven, that in respect of the talking of the joys thereof all worldly recreation be but a grief to think on.   And be sure, Cousin, that if we might once purchase the grace to come to that point, we never found of worldly recreation so much comfort in a year, as we should find in the bethinking us of heaven in less than half-an-hour."[1]

From the above quotations, it will be seen that the question of facetious writing is very much narrowed, when it is considered in relation to Sir Thomas More.   In his youth he loved epigrams.   It was a period when the scholars of the Renaissance were copying the obscenity no less than the wit of their heathen models.   From this vice young More carefully abstained, though a few trifles have been printed against his will, which he afterwards regretted.[2] In his early manhood he translated three of Lucian's dialogues, which he especially admired for their wit as well as for their matter.   He was ever fond of a joke.   In 1508, when he was thirty years old, Erasmus calls him *insignis nugator*, a famous lover of fun.   His humour brightens up his most serious controversial writings, and gives a flavour to his ascetic treatises which few (I think) can fail to relish.

Erasmus, who lived long in Blessed More's house, and was his dearest friend, says that his handsome face

---

[1] *Dialogue of Comfort*, Works, 1171.

[2] "You know," he says in a letter to Erasmus, "that when my epigrams were being printed, I did all I could to suppress those that might be personal, as well as a few that did not seem to me serious enough : quod quædam mihi non satis severa videbantur, etiamsi procul absint ab ea obscœnitate, qua ferme sola quorumdam epigrammata video commendari." (*T. Mori Lucubrationes*, p. 435. Ed. 1563.)

seemed always ready for mirth ; but that his fun was self-contained, not noisy, and never uncharitable, never bitter, and never verged on scurrility or buffoonery. He describes him as a man who could be all to all men, whose company, whose look, whose conversation increased joy, dissipated dulness, and soothed sorrow. Such a character cannot be illustrated by relating a few *bon mots* or pleasant sayings. It is only by reading his works that any adequate conception can be formed of his deep wisdom and brilliant wit, his lively fancy, his richness of illustration, his shrewdness, his clever turns of expression, his homely, forcible words, his light banter, or his scathing sarcasm. His life as related by his contemporaries, and his writings, show throughout a strange yet beautiful mixture of joyousness and seriousness, of almost boyish fun and altogether saintly earnestness, of gentle merriment and tender pathos, of unfaltering confidence in God united with awe and adoration of His majesty and justice. We must not think of him for a moment as a jocose man, a jester, or a punster. Now and then, indeed, his wit will play upon words, but generally it is busied with deeper things than external forms. All are familiar with the quaint sayings uttered by him at the scaffold. It was these that gave occasion to Hall, the chronicler and panegyrist of the stupid pageantries in which Henry VIII. so delighted, to accuse Henry's victim of buffoonery ; and some dull historians have not known whether to admire his intrepidity or be shocked at his levity. They must know little of his character or of the facts of his life who speak of levity in connection with his heroic death. Such men would doubtless call the conduct of Elias levity, when, after his fast of forty days, he summoned the prophets and priests of the idol Baal to meet him on Mount Carmel, and mocked their prayers. " Cry with a louder voice ; for he is a god, and perhaps he is talking, or at an inn, or on a journey, or is asleep and must be waked." [1]

Let us examine a little these levities of Blessed Thomas. During his fifteen months' imprisonment in the Tower he had prepared himself in prayer, and fasting, and hair-shirt for his death. He had had—as we know from his own testimony—many a night of agony, when he thought, not so much of his own end as of the distress and temporal ruin that his refusal of the oath was bringing on his wife and children. His meditations were on the agony of our Lord in the Garden, on which he composed a most affecting treatise. He had fought his battle and gained his victory. He had been strengthened by his angel in his weakness, and at the end all weakness had passed away. He had committed his family to God, and the summons to die was to him a glad message of release—a call of the Bridegroom to His heavenly banquet. He went towards the scaffold with a light heart. The ladder was unsteady and he was weak with long sickness and imprisonment. Turning to the lieutenant of the Tower, who accompanied him, he said : " I pray thee see me safe up, and for my coming down let me shift for myself ". Levity ! Say rather the elasticity of a heavenly heart, as the weary feet began to mount the ladder of heaven. His prayer on the scaffold was the psalm *Miserere*, the penitent's psalm. When it was said, and he had spoken his few words to the people, declaring his loyalty both to his king and his God, he laid his head upon the block. " Wait," he said, half to

[1] 3 Kings xviii. 27.

himself, half to the executioner; "let me move aside my
beard before you strike, for that has at least committed no
treason." Levity again! Say rather the scorn of a loyal
heart at being condemned to a traitor's death. These playful sayings were neither buffooneries nor jokes, but rather
fitting antiphons before and after the psalm of penitence
and hope.

But let us go back from his death to his life, and see what
use he had made of these special gifts, of his peculiar character or temperament. His wit taught him, in the first
place, to strip the mask from the world in which he mixed,
so that it neither dazzled nor seduced him; and, in the
second place, it taught him to strip the mask from the
deadly heresies which arose in his latter days, so that they
became, under his caustic pen, as ridiculous as they were
hateful to the thousands who read his books. (1) First,
then, his wit—not alone, of course, but with prayer, and
meditation, and the grace of God—kept his soul pure from
the seductions of the world. Without any ambition he had
been forced into the life of a court, and had risen from
dignity to dignity. He was constantly in the company of
great men and of princes, in the midst of banquets and
pageantry. Wit gave him a keen insight into the essence of
things, so that pomp and pageantry amused rather than
dazzled him. One who lived with him, Richard Pace, the
king's secretary and Dean of St. Paul's, called him a Demo-
critus, a laughing philosopher. Diplomacy, treaties of peace
and commerce, war and truce, were to him the trifling of
grown-up men, not very much wiser or more serious than
the games of children. His *Utopia* is full of quaint irony
on these matters. His wit even helped him to make light

of imprisonment. So habitually had Blessed Thomas looked on this world as God's prison-house, that when he was actually thrown into prison he could realise no change except that the bounds of his wandering were now somewhat narrower. Thus his wit, that is to say, his deep, subtle, penetrating insight into human life, his amusement at its emptiness and pretence, went along with the grace of God to keep his heart simple, steadfast, undefiled, undeceived in prosperity, undismayed in adversity. (2) Wit also helped Blessed Thomas to strip the mask from heresy. In the latter part of his life he was thrown into controversy with the first Lutheran reformers. Some have accused him of rudeness, and bitterness, and insolence in his manner of conducting this controversy. But they forget the difference between his day and ours. Protestants to us are men and women, erring indeed, yet who may be supposed to be in good faith, since they have been brought up in error, and are confirmed in it by inherited traditions. They deserve, therefore, to be treated courteously and respectfully. Blessed More had to deal with men who were formal heretics, apostates from the Church ; with priests, and monks, and friars who had deserted their altars and their cloisters, and violated their sacred vows. Yet, while they indulged in every kind of licence and neglected every sacred duty, and were fighting against the Holy Ghost, and seeking by every means to destroy the work of our Lord's Precious Blood, they made sanctimonious pretences, quoted unceasingly Holy Scripture, and affected zeal for truth and the glory of God. Simple souls were often deceived by these pretences, not seeing the ravening wolf under the sheep's clothing, dazzled (to use a metaphor of Blessed

More) by the peacock's tail, and not noticing his ugly feet and strident voice. Now Blessed More's shrewdness and fineness of perception not only enabled him to see the true character of this revolt against the Church, but to expose it. He ruthlessly strips off the mask, sometimes with stern indignation, sometimes with biting sarcasm, sometimes with overpowering ridicule. His wit, humour, and power of ridicule saved many an honest man who read his books from becoming a victim of heresy. And let it be said, in passing, that a little of Blessed More's sarcastic spirit is a great help to those who are obliged to mix much with unbelievers and misbelievers, and to hear or read their attacks upon the Catholic Church. It is only when a child comes to the *age of reason* that be begins to approach the tribunal of penance ; when he arrives at the *age of discretion* that he is allowed to kneel at the altar. A further advance is necessary before he can safely read anti-Catholic literature, or mix with mocking heretics. He must have reached the *age of disdain*. Now the age of reason is seven or eight, that of discretion is ten or twelve ; how many years must we count for the age of disdain ? It is not a question of years : some never reach this age ; some are always timorous, overawed by the pretences of heretics—such can never read without danger attacks on Catholic faith or institutions. The age of disdain is when we get a little of the knowledge of the world, the insight into human character, the sarcastic spirit of Blessed Thomas More. This spirit was left as a legacy to the Catholics of England by the martyr-chancellor, and can be traced through all our controversial literature, from Dr. Harding in the days of Elizabeth to Dr. Lingard in our

own days.[1] It has nothing to do with pride or uncharit-
ableness. It is consistent with perfect fairness towards
an adversary. Never was there a fairer controversialist
than Sir Thomas More. Above all, this lofty scorn of
empty pretenders has nothing to do with hatred. Hatred
of any one is inconsistent with charity and humility ; scorn
of falsehood and impiety is simply loyal allegiance to God.

We have seen the uses to which Blessed Thomas put his
natural gifts and character. Let me mention briefly the
dangers to which he was exposed by it, and how he avoided
them. (a) The first danger of a man of keen perception
and sarcastic humour is that of degenerating into a habit of
scoffing and jeering at every man's foible, of suspecting
every man's motives, distrusting all virtue, believing no
man's word, seeing unreality in every noble sentiment or
specious work, imposture in every tale of suffering. Such a
temper is often found in experienced men of the world, and
affected by those who would wish to appear men of the
world. Its motto is *nil admirari*—" to be moved to
admiration by nothing and to be surprised at nothing". It
despises enthusiasm above all things. It is *good form* in
English society among men, and yet it is a detestable
disposition, of which not the least shadow will be found
in Blessed Thomas More. He was preserved from it by
two things especially : by humility, which made him think
little of himself, and keep his own faults and weaknesses
ever before his eyes ; and by charity, which made him look
out for good in others, by charity which " is not puffed up,
rejoiceth not in iniquity, but rejoiceth with the truth". (b)

---

[1] I allude not to his history, but to his tracts, which are very
clever and very pungent.

The second danger to which wit is exposed is that of frivolity, of making light of everything, always seeking out the ridiculous side of things, even in the service and worship of God. There is a good deal of this in certain literature of the present day. Now, piety and reverence for Divine things do not make men affect solemnity in look or tone of voice. Sanctimoniousness, and cant, and religious jargon are offensive to true piety. Blessed Thomas More could make a playful jest about holy things without a touch of profaneness. His faith was so robust, that it had no need to prop itself up with mannerisms and phrases. And if ever there was a man who took not only religious worship, but the whole of life, as a profoundly serious matter, it was the blessed martyr. While other men, even priests and bishops, were making light of taking the oath exacted by the king, Blessed Thomas watched them "playing their pageant," as he called it ; but rather than join them in this pageant, he went to prison and to death. He knew that for every idle word that a man shall speak he shall give an account at the Day of Judgment : and this man of cheerful mirth has left an everlasting example of earnestness in life, of fear of God's judgments and adoration of His holiness. Lastly, there is a word of his that explains best of all how he understood merriment. He used constantly to speak, when taking leave of his friends, of his hopes of being *merry with them with God in heaven.* Heaven to him was merriment, perfect truth, sincerity, innocence, joy in congenial society, above all joy in the source of all genuine and lasting mirth : " Enter thou into the joy of thy Lord ".

PART THE FIRST.

ASCETIC.

ASCETIC.

DIVINE GRACE.

If any man marvel that God made all His creatures such as they should always need aid of His grace, let Him know that God did it out of His double goodness. First, to keep them from pride by causing them [to] perceive their feebleness, [and to call upon Him; and, secondly, to do His creatures honour and comfort. For the creature that wise is can never think himself in so noble condition, nor should take so great pleasure or so much rejoice that he were made able to do a thing well enough himself, as to remember and consider that he hath the most excellent Majesty of God, his Creator and Maker, evermore attendant Himself at his elbow to help him.[1]

CONDITIONS OF OUR REDEMPTION.

God wist that it was nothing meet the servant to stand in better condition than his master. And therefore would He not suffer, that while He came to His own kingdom not without travail and pain, His servants should be slothful and sit and pick their nails, and be carried up to heaven at their ease; but biddeth every man that will be His disciple or servant take up his cross upon his back, and therewith come and follow Him.

And for this cause, too, though the painful Passion of Christ, paid for all mankind, was, of the nature of the thing,

[1] *Treatise on the Passion*, Works, 1285.

(29)

much more than sufficient for the sins of us all, though we
nothing did but sin all our whole life, yet God, not willing
to fill heaven with hell-hounds, limited of His own wisdom
and goodness, after what rate and stint the commodity
thereof should be employed upon us; and ordinarily devised that the merits of His pain taken for us, should make
our labour and pain taken for ourselves meritorious, which
else, had we taken for our sin never so much, and done
never so many good deeds toward the attaining of heaven,
could not have merited us a rush.   And this I say ordinarily; for by special privilege His liberal hand is yet nevertheless at liberty to give remission of sin, and to give grace and
glory where and whensoever He list.[1]

CAUSE OF DULNESS OF FAITH.

Verily, if we would not only lay our ear, but also our
heart thereto, and consider that the saying of our Saviour
Christ is not a poet's fable, nor an harper's song, but the
very holy word of Almighty God Himself, we would, and
well we might, be full sore ashamed in ourselves, and full
sorry too, when we felt in our affection those words to have
in our hearts no more strength and weight, but that we remain still of the same dull mind, as we did before we heard
them.

This manner of ours, in whose breasts the great good
counsel of God no better settleth nor taketh no better root,
may well declare us that the thorns, and the briers, and the
brambles of our worldly substance grow so thick, and spring
up so high in the ground of our hearts, that they strangle, as
the Gospel saith, the word of God that was sown therein.

---

[1] *Treatise on the Passion*, Works, 1290.

And therefore is God very good Lord unto us, when He causeth, like a good husbandman, His folk to come afield (for the persecutors be His folk to this purpose) and with their books and their stocking-irons grub up these wicked weeds and bushes of our earthly substance, and carry them quite away from us, that the word of God sown in our hearts may have room therein, and a glade round about for the warm sun of grace to come to it and make it grow. For surely these words of our Saviour shall we find full true : " Where as thy treasure is, there is also thy heart ".[1]

KNOWLEDGE OF THE SIMPLE.

The name of Housel[2] doth not only signify unto us the blessed Body and Blood of our Lord in the sacramental form, but also—like as this English word God signifieth unto us not only the unity of the Godhead, but also the Trinity of the three Persons, and not only their super-substantial substance, but also every gracious property, as Justice, Mercy, Truth, Almightiness, Eternity, and every good thing more than we can imagine—so doth unto us English folk this English word Housel, though not express yet imply, and under a reverent, devout silence signify, both the sacramental signs and the sacramental things, as well the things contained as the things holily signified, with all the secret unsearchable mysteries of the same. All which holy things right many persons very little learned, but yet in grace godly minded, with heart humble and religious, not arrogant,

---

[1] *Dialogue of Comfort*, Works, 1232.

[2] Housel, the Eucharist, the Holy Communion, etymologically, sacrifice, victim. It was the name always used before the Reformation for the Blessed Sacrament of the altar as received by the faithful.

proud, and curious, under the name of holy Housel, with
inward heavenly comfort, do full devoutly reverence. As
many a good, poor, simple, unlearned soul honoureth God full
devoutly under the name of God, that cannot yet tell such
a tale of God as some great clerks can, that are yet for lack
of like devotion, nothing near so much in God's grace and
favour.[1]

Reserve in Teaching.

If I were again to read in Lincoln's Inn, and there were
in hand with a statute that touched treason and all other
felonies, I would not let to look, seek out, and rehearse,
whether any heinous words spoken against the prince were,
for the only speaking, to be taken for treason or not. Nor
I would not let, in like wise, to declare, if I found out any
cases in which a man, though he took another man's horse
against the law, should yet not be judged for a felon thereby.
And this would I not only be bold there to tell them, but
would also be bold in such French as is peculiar to the
laws of this realm, to leave it with them in writing too.

But yet would I reckon myself sore overseen, if all such
things as I would in that school speak in a " reading," I
would, in English, into every man's hand, put out abroad in
print. For there is no such necessity therein as in the
other. For in the places of court these companies must
needs be taught it, out of which companies they must after
be taken that shall be made judges to judge it. But as for
the common people to be told that tale, shall (as far as I see)
do many folk little good, but rather very great harm. For,
by perceiving that, in some things, were nothing the peril that

[1] *Treatise on the Passion*, Works, 1339.

they feared, some may wax therein more negligent, and by less fearing the less danger may soon step into the more. And therefore have I wist ere this the judges, of a great wisdom, in great open audience, when they have had occasion to speak of high misprision or of treason, forbear yet the inquiry of some such things as they would not have letted to speak among themselves.

If any man would haply think that it were well done that every man were taught all, and would allege therefore that if he knew surely what would make his behaviour high treason or heresy, then, though he would adventure all that ever were under that, yet would he be peradventure the more wary to keep himself well from that ;—as many a man, though he believe he shall abide great pain in purgatory for his venial sins, doth for all that no great diligence in forswearing of them ; and yet, for the fear of perpetual pain in hell taketh very great heed to keep himself from those sins that he surely knoweth for mortal :—

As for such venial sins as folk of frailty so commonly do fall in, that no man is almost any time without them (though the profit would be more if men did ween they were mortal, so that the dread thereof could make men utterly forbear them), yet, since it will not be that men will utterly forbear them, the knowledge of the truth is necessary for them, lest every time that they do such a sin in deed, weening that it were mortal, the doing of the deed, with the conscience of a mortal sin, might make it mortal indeed.

But of any such kind of venial sin as be not so much in custom and may be more easily forborne, I never found any wise man, to my remembrance, that would either write or teach the common people so exactly as to say: " Though you

do thus far, yet is it no deadly sin "; but will in such things
(since the venial sin itself is a drawing toward the deadly)
rather leave the people in doubt and in dread of deadly sin,
and thereby cause them to keep themselves far off from it,
than, by telling them it is but a venial sin, make them the
less afeard to do it, and so come so much the nearer to
mortal sin, and essay how near he can come to it and not
do it, till he come at last so near the brink that his foot
slippeth, and down he falleth into it.　For as the Scripture
sayeth, *Qui amat periculum peribit in illo.*　" He that loveth
peril shall perish in it." [1]

PERSECUTION FOR THE FAITH.

Vincent.—I once heard a right cunning and a very good
man say, that it were great folly, and very perilous too, that
a man should think on what he would do in case of persecution for the faith, or imagine any such case in his mind,
for fear of double peril that may follow thereupon.　For
either shall he be likely to answer himself to the case put by
himself, that he will rather suffer any painful death, than
forsake his faith, and by that bold appointment, should he
fall in the fault of St. Peter that of oversight made a proud
promise, and soon had a foul fall ; or else were he likely to
think that rather than abide the pain, he would forsake God
indeed, and by that mind should he sin deadly through his
own folly, whereas he needeth not, as he that shall peradventure never come in the peril to be put thereunto.
And that therefore it were most wisdom never to think
upon any such case.

Antony.—I believe well, Cousin, that you have heard

---

[1] *Debellation of Salem and Bizance,* Works, 963, 964.

some man that would so say. For I can show almost as
much as that left of a good man and a great solemn doctor
in writing. But yet, Cousin, although I should hap to find
one or two more, as good men and as learned too, that
would both say and write the same, yet would I not fear for
my part to counsel my friend to the contrary. For, Cousin,
if his mind answer him, as St. Peter answered Christ, that he
will rather die than forsake Him, though he say therein more
unto himself, than he should be peradventure able to make
good, if it came to the point, yet perceive I not that he doth
in that thought any deadly displeasure unto God; nor St.
Peter, though he said more than he did perform, yet in his
so saying offended not God greatly neither. But his offence
was, when he did not after so well, as he said before. But
now may this man be likely never to fall in the peril of
breaking that appointment, since of some ten thousand that
so shall examine themselves, never one shall fall in that
peril, and yet to have that good purpose all their life,
seemeth me no more harm the while, than a poor beggar
that hath never a penny, to think that if he had great substance, he would give great alms for God's sake.

But now is all the peril, if the man answer himself, that
he would in such case rather forsake the faith of Christ with
his mouth, and keep it still in his heart, than for the con-
fessing of it to endure a painful death. For by this mind
falleth he in deadly sin, which while he never cometh in the
case indeed, if he never had put himself the case he never
had fallen in. But in good faith methinketh that he who
upon that case put unto himself by himself, will make himself that answer, hath the habit of faith so faint and so cold
that to the better knowledge of himself, and of his necessity

to pray for more strength of grace, he had need to have the
question put him, either by himself or some other man.

Besides this, to counsel a man never to think on the case
is, in my mind, as much reason as the medicine that I have
heard taught one for the toothache, to go thrice about a
churchyard and never think upon a fox-tail. For if the
counsel be not given them, it cannot serve them; and if it
be given them, it must put that point of the matter in their
mind, which by-and-by to reject, and think therein neither
one thing or other, is a thing that may be sooner bidden
than obeyed. I ween also that very few men can escape it,
but that though they would never think thereon by themself, yet in one place or other, where they shall hap to
come in company, they shall have the question by adventure
so proposed and put forth, that like as while he heareth one
talking to him, he may well wink if he will, but he cannot
make himself sleep : so shall he, whether he will or no, think
one thing or other therein.

Finally, when Christ spake so often and so plain of the
matter that every man should upon pain of damnation
openly confess his faith, if men took him and by dread of
death would drive him to the contrary ; it seemeth me in a
manner implied therein that we be bound conditionally to
have evermore that mind, actually sometime, and evermore
habitually, that if the case so should fall, then (with God's
help) so we would. And where they find in the thinking
thereon their hearts shrink in the remembrance of the pain
that their imagination representeth to the mind, then must
they call to mind and remember the great pain and torment that Christ suffered for them, and heartily pray for
grace that if the case should so fall, God should give them

strength to stand. And thus with exercise of such meditation, though men should never stand full out of fear of
falling, yet must they persevere in good hope and in full purpose of standing.

And this seemeth me, Cousin, so far forth the mind, that
every Christian man and woman must needs have, that
methinketh that every curate should often counsel all his
parishioners, and every man and woman, their servants and
their children, even beginning in their tender youth, to know
this point, and to think thereon, and little and little from
their very childhood to accustom them dulcely and pleasantly
in the meditation thereof, whereby the goodness of God shall
not fail so to aspire the grace of His Holy Spirit into their
hearts, in reward of that virtuous diligence, that through such
actual meditation, He shall confirm them in such a sure
habit of spiritual, faithful strength, that all the devils in hell,
with all the wrestling that they can make, shall never be able
to wrest it out of their heart.

Vincent.—By my troth, Uncle, methinketh you say very
well.

Antony.—I say surely, Cousin, as I think. And yet all
this have I said concerning them that dwell in such places,
as they be never like in their lives to come in the danger to
be put to the proof. Howbeit, many a man may ween
himself further therefrom, that yet may fortune by some
one chance or other, to fall in the case that either for the
truth of faith, or for the truth of justice (which go almost
alike) he may fall in the case. But now be you and I,
Cousin, and all our friends here, far in another point. For
we be so likely to fall in the experience thereof so soon, that
it had been more time for us (all other things set aside) to

have devised upon this matter, and firmly to have settled ourselves upon a fast point long ago, than to begin to commune and counsel upon it now.[1]

APOSTASY FROM FEAR OF DEATH.

Vincent.—Every man, Uncle, naturally grudgeth at pain, and is very loath to come to it.

Antony.—That is very truth, nor no man biddeth any man to go run into it. But that if he be taken, and may not flee, then we say that reason plainly telleth us, that we should rather suffer and endure the less and the shorter here, then in hell the sorer, and so far the longer too.

Vincent.—I beard. Uncle, of late, where such a reason was made, as you made me now, which reason seemeth undoubted and inevitable unto me : yet heard I late, as I say. a man answer it thus. He said, that if a man in his persecution should stand still in the confession of his faith, and thereby fall into painful tormentry, he might peradventure hap for the sharpness and bitterness of the pain, to forsake the Saviour even in the midst, and die there with his sin, and so be damned for ever ; whereas, by the forsaking of the faith in the beginning betime, and for the time, and yet not but in word neither, keeping it still, nevertheless, in his heart, a man may save himself from that painful death, and after ask mercy, and have it, and live long, and do many good deeds, and be saved as St. Peter was.

Antony.—That man's reason, Cousin, is like a three-footed stool, so tottering on every side, that whoso sit thereon may soon take a foul fall. For those are the three

---

[1] *Dialogue of Comfort*, Works, 1214.

feet of this tottering stool : fantastical fear, false faith, false
flattering hope.   First, this is a fantastical fear, that the
man conceiveth that it should be perilous to stand in the
confession of the beginning, lest he might afterwards through
the bitterness of pain fall to the forsaking, and so die there
in the pain therewith out of hand, and thereby be utterly
damned : as though that, if a man by pain were overcome,
and so forsook his faith, God could not, or would not, as
well give him grace to repent again, and thereupon give him
forgiveness, as him that forsook his faith in the beginning,
and did set so little by Him, that he would rather forsake
Him than suffer for His safe any manner pain at all : as
though the more pain that a man taketh for God's sake, the
worse would God be to him.   If this reason were not
unreasonable, then should our Saviour not have said, as He
did : " Fear not them that may kill the body, and after that
have nothing that can do farther".   For He should by thi ·
reason have said : " Dread and fear them that may slay the
body ; for they may by the torment of painful death (but
if thou forsake Me betimes in the beginning and so save thy
life, and get of Me thy pardon and forgiveness after) make
thee peradventure forsake Me too late, and so be damned
for ever ".   The second foot of this tottering stool is a false
faith.   For it is but a feigned faith for a man to say to
God secretly that he believeth Him, trusteth Him, and
loveth Him ; and then openly, where he should to God's
honour tell the same tale, and thereby prove that he doth
so, there to God's dishonour (as much as in him is) flatter
God's enemies, and do them pleasure and worldly worship,
with the forsaking of God's faith before the world : and he
is either faithless in his heart too, or else wotteth well that

he doth God this despite, even before His own face. For except he lack faith, he cannot but know that our Lord is everywhere present ; and while he so shamefully forsaketh Him, full angrily looketh on.

The third part of this tottering stool is false, flattering hope. For since the thing that he doth, when he forsaketh his faith for fear, is by the mouth of God (upon the pain of eternal death) forbidden, though the goodness of God forgiveth many folk the fault, yet to be the bolder in offending for the hope of forgiving, is a very false pestilent hope, wherewith a man flattereth himself toward his own destruction. He that in a sudden braid for fear, or other affection unadvisedly falleth, and after in labouring to rise again, comforteth himself with hope of God's gracious forgiveness, walketh in the ready way towards his salvation. But he that, with the hope of God's mercy to follow, doth encourage himself to sin, and therewith offendeth God first (I have no power to shut the hand of God from giving out His pardon where He list, nor would, if I could, but rather help to pray therefor, but yet) I very sore fear, that such a man may miss the grace to require it in such effectual wise, as to have it granted. Nor I cannot suddenly now remember any sample or promise expressed in Holy Scripture, that the offender in such a kind shall have the grace offered after in such wise to seek for pardon, that God hath (by His other promises of remission promised to the penitents) bound Himself to grant it. But this kind of presumption under pretext of hope, seemeth rather to draw near on the one side as despair doth on the other side, toward the abominable sin of blasphemy against the Holy Ghost. Against which sin concerning either the impossibility, or, at

the least, the great difficulty of forgiveness, our Saviour saith
that blasphemy against the Holy Ghost shall never be
forgiven, neither in this world nor in the world to come.

And where the man that you spake of, took in his reason
a sample of St. Peter which forsook our Saviour, and gat
forgiveness after ; let him consider again on the other side,
that he forsook Him not upon the boldness of any such
sinful trust, but was overcome and vanquished upon a sudden
fear. And yet by that forsaking St. Peter won but little.
For he did but delay his trouble for a little while, you wot
well. For beside that he repented forthwith very sore that
he so had done, and wept therefor by-and-by full bitterly,
he came forth at the Whitsuntide ensuing, and confessed
his Master again, and soon after that he was imprisoned
therefor : and not ceasing so, was thereupon scourged for
the confession of his faith, and yet after that imprisoned
again afresh ; and being from thence delivered, stinted not
to preach on still, until that after manifold labours, marvels,
and troubles, he was at Rome crucified, and with cruel
torment slain. And in likewise I ween, I might in a
manner well warrant that there shall no man (which denieth
our Saviour once, and after attaineth remission) scape
through that denying, one penny the better cheap, but that
he shall, ere he come in heaven, full surely pay therefor.

Vincent.—He shall peradventure, Uncle, work it out afterwards, in the fruitful works of penance, prayer, and alms-
deeds done in true faith, and due charity, and attain in such
wise forgiveness well enough.

Antony.—All his forgiveness goeth, Cousin, you see well,
but by perhaps. But as it may be, perhaps yea : so it may
be, perhaps nay. And where is he then? And yet you

wot well, by no manner hap he shall never hap finally to scape from death, for fear of which he forsook his faith.

Vincent.—No, but he may die his natural death, and scape that violent death, and then he saveth himself from much pain, and so winneth therewith much ease. For evermore a violent death is painful.

Antony.—Peradventure he shall not avoid a violent death thereby. For God is without doubt displeased, and can bring him shortly to a death as violent by some other way. Howbeit, I see well that you reckon that whoso dieth a natural death, dieth like a wanton even all at his ease. You make me remember a man that was once in a galley-suttle with us on the sea, which while the sea was sore wrought, and the waves rose very high, and he came never on the sea afore, and lay tossed hither and thither, the poor soul groaned sore, and for pain he thought he would very fain be dead, and ever he wished, Would God I were on land, that I might die in rest! The waves so troubled him there with tossing him up and down, to and fro, that he thought that trouble letted him to die, because the waves would not let him rest: but if he might get once to land, he thought he should then die there even at his ease.

Vincent.—Nay, Uncle, this is no doubt, but that death is to every man painful. But yet is not the natural death so painful as the violent.

Antony.—By my troth, Cousin, methinketh that the death which men call commonly natural is a violent death to every man whom it fetcheth hence by force against his will, and that is every man which, when he dieth, is loath to die, and fain would yet live longer if he might. Howbeit, how small the pain is in the natural death, Cousin, fain would I wit

who hath told you. As far as I can perceive, those folk
that commonly depart of their natural death have ever one
disease and sickness or other, whereof if the pain of the
whole week or twain, in which they lie pining in their bed,
were gathered together into so short a time, as a man hath
his pain that dieth a violent death; it would, I ween, make
double the pain that it is. So that he that naturally dieth,
oftener suffereth more pain than less, though he suffer it in
a longer time. And then would many a man be more loath
to suffer so long in lingering pain than with a sharper to be
sooner rid. And yet lieth many a man more days than one
in well near as great pain continually as is the pain that with
the violent death riddeth the man in less than half-an-hour;
except a man would ween that whereas the pain is great, to
have a knife cut his flesh in the outside from the skin
inward, the pain would be much less if the knife might on
the inside begin, and cut from the midst outward. Some
we hear in their death-beds complain that they think they
feel sharp knives cut a-two their heart-strings. Some cry out
and think they feel within the brainpan their head pricked
even full of pins. And they that lie in a pleurisy think that
every time they cough they feel a sharp sword swap them to
the heart.[1]

Christ will have no Half Service.

Vincent.—Yea, I may say to you, I have a motion secretly
made me farther [by the Turk], that is, to wait, not be com-
pelled utterly to forsake Christ, nor all the whole Christian
faith, but only some such parts thereof as may not stand
with Mahomet's law, and only granting Mahomet for a true

[1] *Dialogue of Comfort*, Works, 1254-1256.

prophet, and serving the Turk truly in his wars against all Christian kings, I shall not be letted to praise Christ also, and to call Him a good man, and worship Him and serve Him too.

Antony.—Nay, nay, my lord, Christ hath not so great need of your lordship, as rather than to lose your service, He would fall at such covenants with you, to take your service at halves, to serve Him and His enemy both. He hath given you plam warning already by St. Paul that He will have in your service no parting fellow. "What fellowship is there between light and darkness, between Christ and Belial?" And He hath also plainly showed you Himself by His own mouth: "No man may serve two lords at once". He will have you believe all that He telleth you, and do all that He biddeth you, and forbear all that He forbiddeth you, without any manner exception. Break one of His commandments, and break all. Forsake one point of His faith, and forsake all, as for any thank you get for the remnant. And, therefore, if you devise as it were indentures between God and you, what thing you will do for Him, and what thing you will not do, as though He should hold Him content with such service of yours as yourself list to appoint Him: if you make, I say, such indentures, you shall seal hoth the parts yourself, and you get thereto none agreement of Him.[1]

TRUST IN GOOD WORKS.

Tindale proveth that the Pope believeth not to be saved

[1] *Dialogue of Comfort*, Works, 1228. More adds that to deny Christ to be God is to deny Him altogether, "for surely if He were not God, He were no good man neither, while He plainly said He was God". (1229, A.)

through Christ, because he teacheth to trust in holy works for remission of sins and salvation.

Is not here a perilous lesson, trow ye? namely, so taught as the Church teacheth it, that no good work can be done without help of God's grace; nor no good work of man worthy the reward of heaven, but by the liberal goodness of God; nor yet should have such a price set upon it save through the merits of Christ's bitter passion, and that yet in all our deeds we be so imperfect that each man hath good cause to fear for his own part lest his best be bad.

I would ween that good works were not so deadly poison, but (taking not too much at once, for dosing of the stomach, no more at once, lo! than I see the world wont to do), many drams of such treacle, mixed with one scruple of dread, were able enough, for aught I can see, to preserve the soul from presumption, that one spoonful of good works should no more kill the soul than a potager of good worts kill or destroy the body.[1]

PRESUMPTION AND DESPAIR.

I grant that hope dieth not always with sin, but it waxeth by Tindale's doctrine oftentimes over great. For, by the dreadless trust of their teaching, the man falleth into boldness of sin. In which, when he hath fearless long continued, he waxeth careless, and setteth not by sin, till suddenly the devil, out of his high heart and hault courage, striketh him into cowardous dread and utter desperation. For the outrageous increase of their hope is no very right hope, though it be a greater hope than it should be, no more than the heat of a fever is a right natural heat, though the body

[1] *Confutation of Tindale*, Works, 617,

be more hot than it was in health.   And, therefore, in such
affections the soul sometimes falleth from one contrary
quality into another, as the body in an ague changeth from
cold to heat, and from heat sometimes to cold again.[1]

HOPE OF DEATH-BED REPENTANCE.

Remember, that into God's vineyard there goeth no man,
but he that is called thither.   Now, he that in hope to be
called toward night, will sleep out the morning, and drink
out the day, is full likely to pass at night unspoken to, and
then shall he with shrewd rest go supperless to bed.

They tell of one that was wont alway to say, that all the
while he lived he would do what he list, for three words,
when he died, should make all safe enough.   But then so
happed it, that long ere he were old, his horse once
stumbled upon a broken bridge, and as he laboured to
recover him, when he saw it would not be, but down into
the flood headlong needs he should : in a sudden fright he
cried out in the falling: " Have all to the devil ! "   And
there was he drowned with his three words ere he died,
whereon his hope hung all his wretched life.   And, therefore, let no man sin in hope of grace : for grace cometh but
at God's will, and that mind may be the let, that grace of
fruitful repenting shall never after be offered him, but that
he shall either graceless go, linger on careless, or with a care
fruitless, fall into despair.[2]

RELAPSE.

Christ hath by His death paid every man's ransom, and

[1] *Confutation of Tindale*, Works, 572.
[2] *Dialogue of Comfort*, Works, 1174.

hath delivered us if we will, though many men there be that will not take the benefit thereof. But some will needs lie still in prison, and some will needs thither again, as no man can keep some thieves out of Newgate ; but let them be pardoned and their fees paid, and themselves set on free-foot, and delivered out, yet will they there for good company tarry loose with their fellows awhile, and, before that next Sessions come, sit as fast there as ever they sat before.[1]

REMEDY WHEN SORROW LACKETH.

Vincent.—Of truth some man cannot be sorry and heavy for his sin, though he never so fain would. For, though he can be content for God's sake, to forbear it from henceforth, yet for every sin that is passed can he not only not weep, but some [sins] were haply so wanton that when he happeth to remember them, he can scarcely forbear to laugh. Now, if contrition and sorrow of heart be requisite of necessity to remission, many a man should stand, as it seemeth, in a very perilous case.

Antony.—Many so should indeed, Cousin, and indeed. many so do. And the old saints write very sore in this point. Howbeit "the mercy of God is above all His works," and He standeth bound to no common rule. *Et ipse cognovit figmentum suum, et propitiatur infirmitatibus nostris ;* "and He knoweth the frailty of this earthen vessel that is of His own making, and is merciful, and hath pity and compassion upon our feeble infirmities," and shall not exact of us above that thing that we may do.

But yet, Cousin, he that findeth himself in that case, in

---

[1] *Confutation of Tindale*, Works, 743.

that he is minded to do well hereafter, let him give God thanks that he is no worse : but in that he cannot be sorry for his sin past, let him be sorry hardily that he is no better. And as St. Jerome biddeth him that for his sin sorroweth in his heart, be glad and rejoice in his sorrow : so would I counsel him that cannot be sad for his sin, to be sorry yet at the least that he cannot be sorry.

Besides this, though I would in nowise any man should despair, yet would I counsel such a man, while that affection lasteth, not to be too hold of courage, but live in double fear. First, for it is a token either of faint faith, or of a dull diligence. For surely if we believe in God, and therewith deeply consider His High Majesty with the peril of our sin, and the great goodness of God also : either should dread make us tremble and break our stony heart, or love should for sorrow relent it into tears. Besides this, I can scant believe, but since so little misliking of our old sin is an affection not very pure and clean, and none unclean thing shall enter into heaven ; cleansed shall it be and purified, before that we come there. And, therefore, would I farther advise one in that case, the counsel which M. Gerson giveth every man, that since the body and the soul together make the whole man, the less affliction that he feeleth in his soul, the more pain in recompense let him put upon his body, and purge the spirit by the affliction of the flesh. And he that so doth, I dare lay my life, shall have his hard heart after relent into tears, and his soul in an unwholesome heaviness and heavenly gladness too, specially if, which must be joined with every good thing, he join faithful prayer therewith.[1]

[1] *Dialogue of Comfort*, Works, 1176.

SCRUPULOSITY.

Pusillanimity bringeth forth a very timorous daughter, a silly, wretched girl, and ever puling, that is called Scrupulosity or a scrupulous conscience. This girl is a meetly good puzzle in a house, never idle, but ever occupied and busy; but albeit she have a very gentle mistress that loveth her well, and is well content with that she doth, or if it be not all well (as all cannot be well always), content to pardon her as she doth other of her fellows, and so letteth her know that she will; yet can this peevish girl never cease whining and puling for fear lest her mistress be always angry with her, and that she shall shrewdly be shent. Were her mistress, ween you, like to be content with this condition? Nay, surely. I knew such one myself, whose mistress was a very wise woman, and (which thing is in women very rare) very mild and also meek, and liked very well such service as she did her in the house, but this continual discomfortable fashion of hers she so much misliked, that she would sometimes say: "Eh! what aileth this girl? The elvish urchin weeneth I were a devil, I trow. Surely if she did me ten times better service than she doth, yet with this fantastical fear of hers I would be loath to have her in my house."

Thus fareth the scrupulous person, which frameth himself many times double the fear that he hath cause, and many times a great fear where there is no cause at all, and of that which is indeed no sin, maketh a venial, and that that is venial, imagineth to be deadly. And yet for all that, falleth in them, being namely such of their own nature as no man long liveth without. And then he feareth that he be never full confessed, nor never full contrite, and then that his sins

be never full forgiven him ; and then he confesseth, and confesseth again, and cumbereth himself and his confessor both ;
and then every prayer that he saith, though he say it as well
as the frail infirmity of the man will suffer, yet is he not
satisfied, but if he say it again, and yet after that again.
And when he hath said one thing thrice, as little is he satisfied with the last as with the first ; and then is his heart
evermore in heaviness, unquiet, and in fear, full of doubt
and dulness, without comfort or spiritual consolation.

. . . Let them, therefore, that are in the troublous fear of their
own scrupulous conscience submit the rule of their own
conscience to the counsel of some other good man, which,
after the variety and the nature of the scruples, may temper
his advice. Yea, although a man be very well learned himself, yet let him in this case learn the custom used among
physicians. For be one of them never so cunning, yet in
his own disease and sickness he never useth to trust all to
himself, but sendeth for such of his fellows as he knoweth
meet and putteth himself in their hands, for many con-
siderations, whereof they assign the causes. And one of the
causes is fear, whereof upon some tokens he may conceive
in his own passion a great deal more than needeth ; and
then were it good for his health, that for the time he knew
no such thing at all. I knew once in this town one of the
most cunning men in that faculty, and the best expert, and
therewith the most famous too, and he that the greatest cures
did upon other men, and yet when he was himself once very
sore sick, I heard his fellows that then looked unto him, of
all which every one would, in their own disease, have used
his help before any other man, wish yet that for the time of
his own sickness, being so sore as it was, he had known no

physic at all, he took so great heed unto every suspicious token, and feared so far the worst, that his fear did him sometime much more harm than the sickness gave him cause.

And, therefore, as I say, whoso hath such a trouble of his scrupulous conscience, let him for a while forbear the judgment of himself, and follow the counsel of some other, whom he knoweth for well learned and virtuous, and specially in the place of confession (for there is God specially present with His grace, assisting His holy sacrament), and let him not doubt to acquiet his mind, and follow that he there is bounden, and think for a while less of the fear of God's justice, and be more merry in the remembrance of His mercy, and persevere in prayer for grace, and abide and dwell faithfully in the sure hope of His help.[1]

MAY WE SEEK TO REMOVE CROSSES?

I think in very deed tribulation so good and profitable, that I should haply doubt wherefore a man might labour or pray to be delivered of it, saving that God, which teacheth us the one, teacheth us also the other. And as He biddeth us take our pain patiently, and exhort our neighbours to do also the same ; so biddeth He us also not to let to do our devoir to remove the pain from us both. And then when it is God that teacheth both, I shall not need to break my brain in devising wherefore He would bid us do both, the one seeming to resist the other. If He send the scourge of scarcity and of famine, He will we shall bear it patiently, but yet will He that we shall eat our meat when we can hap to get it. If He send us the plague of pestilence, He will

[1] *Dialogue of Comfort*, Works, 1182, 1186.

that we shall patiently take it ; but yet will He that we let
us blood, and lay plasters to draw it, and ripe it, and lance
it, and get it away.   Both these points teacheth God in
Scripture in more than many places.   Fasting is better than
eating, and more thank hath of God ; and yet will God
that we shall eat.   Praying is better than drinking, and
much more pleasant to God ; and yet will God that we
shall drink.   Waking in good business is much more
acceptable to God than sleeping ; and yet will God that we
shall sleep.

God have given us our bodies here to keep, and will that
we maintain them to do Him service with, till He send for
us hence.   Now, can we not tell surely how much tribulation may mar it, or peradventure hurt the soul also ?
Wherefore the apostle, after that he had commanded the
Corinthians to deliver to the devil the abominable fornicator
that forbare not the bed of his own father's wife : yet after
that he had been awhile accursed and punished for his sin,
the apostle commanded them charitably to receive him
again and give him consolation, "that the greatness of his
sorrow should not swallow him up ".   And, therefore, when
God sendeth the tempest, He will that the shipmen shall
get them to their tackling, and do the best they can for
themselves, that the sea eat them not up.   For help ourselves as well as we can, He can make His plague as sore,
and as long lasting, as Himself list.   And as He will that
we do for ourselves, so will He that we do for our
neighbour too : and that we shall in this world be each to
other piteous, and not *sine affectione*, for which the apostle
rebuketh them that lack their tender affections here, so that
of charity sorry should we be for their pain too, upon whom

(for cause necessary) we be driven ourselves to put it. And whoso saith, that for pity of his neighbour's soul he will have none of his body, let him be sure that (as St. John saith, he that loveth not his neighbour whom he seeth, loveth God but a little whom he seeth not) : so he that hath no pity on the pain that he seeth his neighbour feel afore him, pitieth little (whatsoever he say) the pain of his soul that he seeth not yet.

God sendeth us also such tribulation sometime, because His pleasure is to have us pray unto Him for help. And, therefore, when St. Peter was in prison, the Scripture showeth that the whole Church without intermission prayed incessantly for him ; and that at their fervent prayer God by miracle delivered him. When the disciples in the tempest stood in fear of drowning, they prayed unto Christ and said : " Save us, Lord, we perish ". And then at their prayer He shortly ceased the tempest. And now see we proved often, that in sore weather or sickness, by general processions God giveth gracious help. And many a man in his great pain and sickness, by calling upon God, is marvellously made whole. This is God's goodness, that because in wealth we remember Him not, but forget to pray to Him, sendeth us sorrow and sickness to force us to draw toward Him, and compelleth us to call upon Him and pray for release of our pain. Whereby when we learn to know Him, and seek to Him, we take a good occasion to fall after into farther grace.[1]

WE KNOW NOT WHAT TO ASK.

How many men attain health of body, that were better

[1] *Dialogue of Comfort*, Works, 1160.

for their souls' health their bodies were sick still ! How
many get out of prison, that hap on such harm abroad as
the prison should have kept them from ! How many that
have been loth to lose their worldly goods have in keeping
of their goods soon after lost their lives ! So blind is our
mortality and so unaware what will fall, so unsure also what
manner of mind we will ourselves have to-morrow, that God
could not lightly do man a more vengeance than in this
world to grant him his own foolish wishes. What wit have
we (poor fools) to wit what will serve us, when the blessed
apostle himself in his sore tribulation, praying thrice unto
God to take it away from him, was answered again by God
in a manner that he was but a fool in asking that request,
but that the help of God's grace in that tribulation to
strengthen him was far better for him, than to take the
tribulation from him ? And, therefore, by experience
perceiving well the truth of that lesson, he giveth us good
warning not to be bold of our own minds when we require
aught of God, nor to be precise in our asking, but refer the
choice to God at His own pleasure. For His own Holy
Spirit so sore desireth our weal, that, as men might say, He
groaneth for us in such wise as no tongue can tell. "We,
what we may pray for that were behoveable for us, cannot
ourself tell (saith St. Paul) : but the Spirit Himself desireth
for us with unspeakable groanings."

And, therefore, I say, for conclusion of this point, let us
never ask of God precisely our own ease by delivery from
our tribulation, but pray for His aid and comfort, by which
ways Himself shall best like ; and then may we take
comfort, even of our such request. For both be we sure
that this mind cometh of God, and also be we very sure

that as He beginneth to work with us, so (but if ourselves
flit from Him) He will not fail to tarry with us ; and then,
He dwelling with us, what trouble can do us harm ?   " If
God be with us (saith St. Paul), who can stand against
us ? " [1]

PRIDE.

If it be so sore a thing and so far unfitting in the sight of
God to see the sin of pride in the person of a great estate,
and that hath yet many occasions of inclination thereunto ;
how much more abominable is that peevish pride in a lewd,
unthrifty javell that hath a purse as penniless as any poor
pedlar, and bath yet a heart as high as many a mighty
prince.   And if it be odious in the sight of God that a
woman beautiful indeed abuse the pride of her beauty to the
vain glory of herself; how delectable is that dainty damsel to
the devil, that standeth in her own light and taketh herself
for fair, weening herself well liked for her broad forehead,
while the young man that beholdeth her marketh more her
crooked nose.

And if it be a thing detestable for any creature to rise in
pride upon the respect and regard of personage, beauty,
strength, wit, or learning, or other such manner thing as by
nature and grace are properly their own, how much more
foolish abusion is there in that pride by which we worldly
folk look up on high, solemnly set by ourselves, with deep
disdain of other far better men, only for very vain, worldly
trifles that properly be not our own.   How proud be men of
gold and silver, no part of ourself but of the earth, and of
nature no better than is the poor copper or tin, nor to man's
use so profitable as is the poor metal that maketh us the

----

[1] *Dialogue of Comfort*, Works, 1147.

ploughshare and the horseshoe and horse-nails. How
proud be many men of these glistering stones, of which the
very brightness, though it cost thee £20, shall never shine
half as bright, nor show thee half so much light, as shall a
poor halfpenny candle. How proud is many a man over his
neighbour because the wool of his gown is finer, and yet, as
fine as it is, a poor sheep wore it on her back before it came
on his, and all the time she wore it, were her wool never so
fine, yet was she, pardie! but 'a sheep. And why should
he be now better than she by that wool, that, though it
be his, is yet not so verily his as it was verily hers? But
now, how many men are there proud of that that is not theirs
at all! Is there no man proud of keeping another man's
gate? another man's horse? another man's hound or hawk?
What a bragging maketh a bearward with his silver-buttoned
baudrick for pride of another man's bear!

Howbeit what speak we of other men's and our own? I
can see nothing (the thing well weighed) that any man may
well call his own. But as men may call him a fool that
heareth himself proud because he jetteth about in a borrowed gown, so may we be well called very fools all, if we
hear us proud of anything that we have here. For nothing
have we here of our own, not so much as our own bodies,
but have borrowed it all of God, and yield it we must
again, and send our silly soul out' naked, no man can tell
how soon. . . . For all these must we depart from every
whit again, except our soul alone. And yet that must we
give God again also, or else shall we keep it still with such
sorrow, as we were better lose it.

I counsel every man and woman to beware even of the
very least spice of pride, which seemeth to be the bare

delight and liking of ourselves, for anything that either is in
us or outwardly belonging to us.   Let us every man lie well
in wait of ourselves, and let us mark well when the devil first
casteth any proud, vain thought into our mind, and let us
forthwith make a cross on our breast, and bless it out by-
and-by, and cast it at his head again.   For if we gladly take
in one such guest of his, he shall not fail to bring in two of
his fellows soon after, and every one worse than [the] other.
This point expresseth well the Spirit of God by the mouth
of the prophet, where he noteth the perilous progress of
proud folk, in the person of whom he saith in this wise:
*Dixerunt ; Linguam nostram magnificabimus, labia nostra a
nobis sunt, quis noster dominus est ?*   They have said:
" We will magnify our tongues, our lips be our own, who is
our lord?"   First they begin, lo ! but as it were with a vain
delight and pride of their own eloquent speech, and say
they will set it out goodly to the show ; wherein yet seemeth
little harm, save a fond foolish vanity, if they went no
farther.   But the devil that bringeth them to that point
first intendeth not to suffer them to rest and remain there,
but shortly he maketh them think and say farther: *Labia
nostra a nobis sunt,* " Our lips be our own, we have them of
ourselves".   At what point are they now, lo !   Do they not
now the thing that God hath lent them take for their own,
and will not be aknowen that it is His?   Thus become they
thieves unto God.   And yet the devil will not leave them
thus neither, but carrieth them forth farther unto the very
worst point of all.   For when they say once that their lips
be their own and of themselves, then against the truth that
they have their lips lent them of our Lord, their prone
hearts arise and they ask : *Quis noster dominus est ?*   " Who

is our lord?" And so deny that they have any lord at all.
And then, lo! beginning but with a vain pride of their own
praise, they become secondly thieves unto God, and finally
from thieves they fall to be plain rebellious traitors, and
refuse to take God for their God, and fall into the detestable
pride that Lucifer fell to himself.[1]

AMBITION.

As for fame and glory, desired but for worldly pleasure,
it doth unto the soul inestimable harm. For that setteth
men's hearts upon high devices and desires of such things
as are immoderate and outrageous, and by the help of false
flatteries puff up a man in pride, and make a brittle man
lately made of earth, and that shall again shortly be laid
full low in earth, and there lie and rot, and turn again into
earth, take himself in the meantime for a god here upon
earth, and ween to win himself to be lord of all the earth.
This maketh battles between these great princes, and with
much trouble to much people and great effusion of blood,
one king to look to reign in five realms that cannot well rule
one. For how many hath now this great Turk, and yet
aspireth to more? And those that he hath he ordereth
evil, and yet himself worse.

Then offices and rooms of authority, if men desire them
only for their worldly phantasies, who can look that ever
they shall occupy them well, but abuse their authority, and
do thereby great hurt? For then shall they fall from
indifferency and maintain false matters of their friends,
bear up their servants, and such as depend upon them, with

---

[1] *Treatise on the Passion*, Works, 1272.

bearing down of other innocent folk, and not so able to do hurt as easy to take harm.

Then the laws that are made against malefactors shall they make, as an old philosopher said, to be much like unto cobwebs, in which the little gnats and flies stick still and hang fast, but the great humble bees break them and fly quite through. And then the laws that are made as a buckler in the defence of innocents, those shall they make serve for a sword to cut and sore wound them with, and therewith wound they their own souls sorer.[1]

AVARICE.

I remember me of a thief once cast at Newgate, that cut a purse at the bar when he should be hanged on the morrow. And when he was asked why he did so, knowing that he should die so shortly, the desperate wretch said that it did his heart good to be lord of that purse one night yet. And in good faith, methinketh, as much as we wonder at him, yet we see many that do much like, of whom we nothing wonder at all. I let pass old priests that sue for vowsons of younger priests' benefices. I let pass old men that gape to be executors to some that be younger than themselves, whose goods, if they would fall, they reckon would do them good to have in their keeping yet one year ere they died. But look if ye see not some wretch that scant can creep for age, his head hanging in his bosom, and his body crooked, walk pit-pat upon a pair of pattens, with the staff in the one hand and the Paternoster[2] in the other hand, the one foot almost in the grave already, and yet never the more haste to part with anything, nor to restore that he hath

---

[1] *Dialogue of Comfort*, Works, 1226. [2] Rosary beads.

evil gotten, but as greedy to get a groat by the beguiling of his neighbour, as if he had of certainty seven score year to live.[1]

How a Rich Man May Remain Humble.

Antony.—Let him think in his own heart every poor beggar his fellow.

Vincent.—That will be very hard, Uncle, for an honourable man to do, when he beholdeth himself richly apparelled, and the beggar rigged in his rags.

Antony.—If here were, Cousin, two men that were beggars both, and afterward a great rich man would take the one unto him, and tell him that for a little time he would have him in his house, and thereupon arrayed him in silk, and gave him a great bag by his side filled even full of gold, but giving him this knot therewith, that within a little while out he should in his old rags again, and bear never a penny with him. If this beggar met his fellow now, while his gay gown were on, might he not for all his gay gear take him for his fellow still ? And were he not a very fool, if for a wealth of a few weeks he would ween himself far his better ?

Vincent.—Yes, by my troth, Uncle, if the difference of their state were none other.

Antony.—Surely, Cousin, methinketh that in this world between the richest and the most poor the difference is scant so much. For let the highest look on the most base, and consider how poor they came both into this world, and then consider farther therewith how rich soever he be now, he shall yet within a while, peradventure less than one

[1] *Four Last Things*, Works, 94.

week, walk out again as poor as that beggar shall ; and then, by my troth, methinketh this rich man much more than mad, if for the wealth of a little while, haply less than one week, he reckon himself in earnest any better than the beggar's fellow. And less than this can no man think that hath any natural wit, and well useth it.

But now a Christian man, Cousin, that hath the light of faith, cannot fail to think in this thing much farther. For he will think not only upon his bare coming hither, and his bare going hence again, but also upon the dreadful judgment of God, and upon the fearful pains of hell, and the inestimable joys of heaven. And in the considering of these things he will call to remembrance that, peradventure, when this beggar and he be both departed hence, the beggar may be suddenly set up in such royalty that well were himself that ever he was born if he might be made his fellow.[1]

Bear no Malice.

Bear no malice nor evil will to no man living. For, either that man is good or naught.[2] If he be good, and I hate him, then am I naught. If he be naught, either he shall amend and die good and go to God, or abide naught and die naught, and go to the devil. And then let me remember that, if he shall be saved, he shall not fail, if I be saved too, as I trust to be, to love me very heartily, and I shall then in likewise love him. And why should I now, then, hate one for this while, which shall hereafter love me for evermore ? And why should I be now, then, enemy to him, with whom I shall in time coming be coupled in eternal friendship ? Or, on the other side, if he shall continue

---

[1] *Dialogue of Comfort*, Works, 1201.   [2] Wicked.

naught and be damned, then is there so outrageous eternal
sorrow towards him,[1] that I may well think myself a deadly
cruel wretch if I would not now rather pity his pain than
malign his person.

If one would say that we may well, with good conscience,
wish an evil man harm, lest he should do harm to such
other folk as are innocent and good, I will not now dispute
upon that point, for that root hath more branches to be
well weighed and considered, than I can now conveniently
write, having none other pen than a coal.[2]   But verily thus
will I say, that I will give counsel to every good friend of
mine, but[3] if he be put in such room, as to punish
an evil man lieth in his charge by reason of his office, else
leave the desire of punishing unto God, and unto such other
folk as are so grounded in charity, and so fast, cleave to
God, that no secret, shrewd, cruel affection, under the cloak
of a just and virtuous seal, can creep in and undermine
them.   But let us that are no better than men of a mean
sort, ever pray for such merciful amendment in other folk, as
our own conscience showeth us that we have need in our
self.[4]

SLANDER OF CLASSES.

Those that be spiritual persons by profession, and are
therewith carnal and wretched in their condition, have never
been favoured by me.   But I perceive well that these good
brethren look that I should rebuke the clergy and seek out

---

[1] To come upon him.

[2] This little meditation was written by the blessed martyr in the
Tower not long before his death.   It shows the feelings he enter-
tained towards his cruel murderer, Henry VIII.

[3] Unless.   [4] Works, 1405.

their faults and lay them to their faces, and write some work
to their shame, or else they cannot call me but partial to the
priests. . . . But surely my guise is not to lay the faults of
the naughty to the charge of any whole company, and rail
upon merchants and call them usurers, nor to rail upon
franklins and call them false jurors, nor to rail upon sheriffs
and call them ravenors, nor to rail upon escheators and call
them extortioners, nor upon all officers and call them
bribers, nor upon gentlemen and call them oppressors, nor
so foolish up higher to call every degree by such odious
names as men might find some of that sort.

And of all degrees, specially for my part, I have ever
accounted my duty to forbear all such manner of un-
mannerly behaviour towards those two most eminent orders
that God hath here ordained on earth, the two great orders,
I mean, of special consecrate persons, the sacred princes and
priests. Against any of which two reverend orders whoso
be so lewd unreverently to speak, and malapertly to jest and
rail, shall play that part alone for me. And rather will I
that these brethren call me partial than for such ill-fashion
indifferent.[1]

The Devil Assists Evil Counsels.

Here we may well consider that when men are in device
about mischief, if they bring their purpose properly to pass
cause have they none to be proud and praise their own wits.
For the devil it is himself that bringeth their matters about,
much more a great deal than they. There was once a
young man fallen in a lewd mind toward a woman, and she
was such as he could conceive no hope to get her, and,

[1] *Apology*, Works, 868.

therefore, was falling to a good point in his own mind to let that lewd enterprise pass. He mishapped, nevertheless, to show his mind to another wretch, which encouraged him to go forward and leave it not. " For, begin thou once, man," quoth he, " and never fear ; let the devil alone with the remnant, he shall bring it to pass in such wise as thyself alone cannot devise how." I trow that wretch had learned that counsel of these priests and these ancients assembled here together against Christ at this council. For here you see that which they were at their wits' end how to bring their purpose about in the taking of Christ, and were at a point to defer the matter and put it over till some other time, the devil sped them by-and-by. For he entered mto Judas' heart, and brought him to them to betray Him forthwith out of hand.[1]

THE BARGAIN OF JUDAS.

" What will ye give me, and I shall deliver Him to you ? " Here shall you see Judas play the jolly merchant, I trow. For he knoweth how fain all this great council would be to have Him delivered. He knoweth well also that it will be hard for any man to deliver Him but one of His own disciples. He knoweth well also, that of all the disciples there would none be so false a traitor to betray his Master but himself alone. "And, therefore, is this ware, Judas, all in thine own hand. Thou hast a monopoly thereof. And while it is so sought for, and so sore desired, and that by so many, and them that are also very rich, thou mayest now make the price of thine own ware thyself, even at thine own pleasure." And, therefore, ye shall, good

[1] *Treatise on the Passion*, Works, 1303.

readers, see Judas wax now a great rich man with this one bargain.

But now the priests and their judges were on the other side covetous too ; and as glad as they were of this ware, yet while it was offered them to sell they thought the merchant was needy, and that to such a needy merchant a little money would be welcome, and money they offered him, but not much. For thirty groats, they said, they will give, which amounteth not much over ten shillings of our English money. Now would we look that the fool would have set up his ware, namely, such ware as it was, so precious in itself that all the money and plate in the whole world were too little to give for it. But now what did the fool ? To show himself a substantial merchant, and not a huckster, he gently let them have it even at their own price.

I wot it well that of the value of the money that Judas had all folk are not of my mind ; but whereas the text saith *triginta argenteos*, some men call *argenteus* a coin of one value and some of another. And some put a difference between *argenteus* and *denarius*, and say that *denarius* is but the tenth part of *argenteus*. But I suppose that *argenteus* was the same silver coin which the Romans at that time used, stamped in silver, in which they expressed the image of the emperor's visage, and the superscription of the emperor's name, and was in Greek called *dragma*, being m weight about the eight part of an ounce. For of such coin there are yet many remaining both of Augustus' days and Tiberius' and of Nero too. So that if the coin were that (for greater silver coin I nowhere find that emperor coined at that time) then was Judas' reward the value of ten shillings of our English money, after the old usual groats used in the time of King Edward III., and long before and long after.[1]

It is a world to mark and consider how the false, wily devil hath in everything that he doth for his servants ever more one point of his envious property, that is to wit, to provide (his sure purpose obtained) that they shall have of his service for their own part as little commodity as he can, even here in this world. For like as he gave here unto Judas no more advantage of his heinous treason but only this poor ten shillings, whereas if his Master Christ had lived, and he still carried His purse, there is no doubt but that he should at sundry times have stolen out for his part far above five times that, so fareth he with all his other servants. Look for whom he doth most in any kind of filthy, fleshly delight, or false, wily winning, or wretched, worldly worship, let him that attaineth it in his unhappy service make his reckoning in the end of all that part, and count well what is come in and what he has payed, that is to wit, lay all his pleasures and his displeasures together, and I dare say he shall find in the end that he had been a great winner if he had never had any of them both. So much grief shall he find himself to have felt far above all his pleasure, even in those days in which his fantasies were in their flowers and prospered, besides the pain and heaviness of heart that now in the end grudgeth and grieveth his conscience, when the time of his pleasure is passed, and the fear of hell followeth at hand.[2]

MUTABILITY OF FAMILIES.

Antony.—Oh! Cousin Vincent, if the whole world were

[1] Sir Thomas was an eager collector of ancient coins.
[2] *Treatise on the Passion*, Works, 1303.

animated with a reasonable soul, as Plato had weened it were, and that it had wit and understanding to mark and perceive all thing: Lord God! how the ground, on which a prince buildeth his palace, would loud laugh his lord to scorn when he saw him proud of his possession, and heard him boast himself that he and his blood are for ever the very lords and owners of that land! For then would the ground think the while in himself: "Oh, thou silly, poor soul, that weenest thou wert half a god, and art amid thy glory but a man in a gay gown: I that am the ground here, over whom thou art so proud, have had an hundred such owners of me as thou callest thyself, more than ever thou hast heard the names of. And some of them that proudly went over my head lie now low in my belly, and my side lieth over them: and many one shall, as thou doest now, call himself mine owner after thee, that neither shall be sib to thy blood, nor any word bear of thy name." Who owned your castle, Cousin, three thousand years ago?

Vincent.—Three thousand, Uncle! Nay, nay, in anything Christian, or heathen, you may strike off a third part of that well enough, and as far as I ween half of the remnant too. In far fewer years than three thousand it may well fortune that a poor ploughman's blood may come up to a kingdom, and a king's right royal kin on the other side fall down to the plough and cart: and neither that king know that ever he came from the cart, nor that carter know that ever he came from the crown.

Antony.—We find, Cousin Vincent, in full authentic stories, many strange chances as marvellous as that, come about in the compass of very few years in effect. And be such things then in reason so greatly to be set by, that we should esteem the loss so great, when we see that in the keeping our surety is so little?[1]

SHORTNESS OF SINFUL PROSPERITY.

Vincent.—God is gracious, and though that men offend him, yet He suffereth them many times to live in prosperity long after.

Antony.—Long after? Nay by my troth, my lord, that doth He no man. For how can that be, that He should suffer you live in prosperity long after, when your whole life is but short in all together, and either almost half thereof, or more than half (you think yourself, I dare say), spent out already before? Can you burn out half a short candle, and then have a long one left of the remnant? There cannot in this world be a worse mind than a man to delight and take comfort in any commodity that he taketh by sinful mean. For it is very straight way toward the taking of boldness and courage in sin, and finally to fall into infidelity, and think that God careth not nor regardeth not what things men do here, nor what mind we be of. But, unto such minded folk speaketh Holy Scripture in this wise: "Say not I have sinned, and yet hath happed me no harm: for God suffereth before He strike". But, as St. Austin saith, the longer that He tarrieth ere He strike, the sorer is the stroke when He striketh. And, therefore, if ye will well do, reckon yourself very sure, that when you deadly displease God for the getting or the keeping of your goods, God shall not suffer those goods to do you good, but either shall He take them shortly from you, or suffer you to keep them for a little while to your more harm : and after shall He, when you

[1] *Dialogue of Comfort*, Works, 1219.

least look therefor, take you away from them. And then
what a heap of heaviness will there enter into your heart,
when you shall see that you shall so suddenly go from your
goods and leave them here in the earth in one place, and
that your body shall be put in the earth in another place:
and (which then shall be most heaviness of all) when you
shall fear (and not without great cause) that your soul shall
first forthwith, and after that (at the final judgment) your
body too, be driven down deep toward the centre of the
earth into the fiery pit and dungeon of the devil of hell,
there to tarry in torment world without end. What goods
of this world can any man imagine, whereof the pleasure and
commodity could be such in a thousand year, as were able
to recompense that intolerable pain that there is to be
suffered in one year, yea, or one day or one hour either?
And then what a madness is it, for the poor pleasure of your
worldly goods of so few years, to cast yourself both body
and soul into the everlasting fire of hell.[1]

DISCOMFORTS OF GREAT MEN.

Goeth all things evermore [with great men] as every one
of them would have it? That were as hard as to please all
the people at once with one weather, while in one house the
husband would have fair weather for his corn, and his wife
would have rain for her leeks. So while they that are in
authority be not all evermore of one mind, but sometime
variance among them, either for the respect of profit, or for
contention of rule, or for maintenance of matters, sundry
parts for their sundry friends: it cannot be that both the
parties can have their own mind, nor often are they content

[1] *Dialogue of Comfort*, Works, 1231.

which see their conclusion quail, but ten times they take the missing of their mind more displeasantly than other poor men do. And this goeth not only to men of mean authority, but unto the very greatest. The princes themselves cannot have, you wot well, all their will. For how were it possible, while each of them almost would, if he might, be lord over all the remnant? Then many men under their princes in authority are in the case, that privy malice and envy many bear them in heart, that falsely speak them fair, and praise them with their mouths, which when their happeth any great fall unto them, bawl, and bark, and bite upon them like dogs.

Finally, the cost and charge, the danger and peril of war, wherein their part is more than a poor man's is, since the matter more dependeth upon them, and many a poor ploughman may sit still by the fire, while they must rise and walk. And sometime their authority falleth by change of their master's mind: and of that see we daily in one place or other ensamples such, and so many, that the parable of the philosopher can lack no testimony, which likened the servants of great princes unto the counters with which men do cast account. For like as that counter that standeth sometime for a farthing, is suddenly set up and standeth for a thousand pound, and after as soon set down, and eftsoon beneath to stand for a farthing again: so fareth it, lo! sometime with those that seek the way to rise and grow up in authority, by the favour of great princes, that as they rise up high, so fall they down again as low.

Howbeit, though a man escape all such adventures, and abide in great authority till he die, yet then at the leastwise every man must leave at the last: and that which we call at

last, hath no very long time to it. Let a man reckon his
years that are passed of his age, ere ever he can get up
aloft; and let him when he hath it first in his fist, reckon
how long he shall be like to live after, and I ween, that then
the most part shall have little cause to rejoice, they shall see
the time likely to be so short that their honour and authority by nature shall endure, beside the manifold chances
whereby they may lose it more soon. And then when they
see that they must needs leave it, the thing which they did
much more set their heart upon, than ever they had reasonable cause: what sorrow they take therefor, that shall I not
need to tell you.

And thus it seemeth unto me, Cousin, in good faith, that
sith in the having the profit is not great, and the displeasures
neither small nor few, and of the losing so many sundry
chances, and that by no mean a man can keep it long, and
that to part therefrom is such a painful grief: I can see no
very great cause, for which, as an high worldly commodity,
men should greatly desire it.[1]

DEATH WATCHES KINGS.

We well know that there is no king so great, but that all
the while he walketh here, walk he never so loose, ride he
with never so strong an army for his defence, yet himself is
very sure (though he seek in the mean season some other
pastime to put it out of his mind)—yet is he very sure, I
say, that scape can he not; and very well he knoweth that
he hath already sentence given upon him to die, and that
verily die he shall, and that himself (though he hope upon
long respite of his execution), yet can he not tell how soon.

[1] *Dialogue of Comfort*, Works, 1225.

And therefore, but if he be a fool, he can never be without
fear, that either on the morrow, or on the selfsame day, the
grisly, cruel hangman, Death, which, from his first coming
in, hath ever hoved aloof, and looked toward him, and ever
lain in await on him, shall amid all his royalty, and all his
main strength, neither kneel before him, nor make him any
reverence, nor with any good manner desire him to come
forth ; but rigorously and fiercely gripe him by the very
breast, and make all his bones rattle, and so by long and
divers sore torments, strike him stark dead, and then cause
his body to be cast into the ground in a foul pit, there to
rot and be eaten with the wretched worms of the earth,
sending yet his soul out farther unto a more fearful judgment, whereof at his temporal death his success is
uncertain.[1]

Unwillingness to Die.

Some are there, I say also, that are loath to die for lack
of wit, which albeit that they believe the world that is to
come, and hope also to come thither, yet they love so much
the wealth of this world, and such things as delight them
therein, that they would fain keep them as long as ever they
might, even with tooth and nail.   And when they may be
suffered in no wise to keep it no longer, but that death
taketh them therefrom ; then if it may be no better, they will
agree to be (as soon as they be hence) hanced up unto
heaven, and be with God by-and-by.   These folk are as
very idiot fools, as he that had kept from his childhood a
bag full of cherrystones, and cast such a phantasy thereto,
that he would not go from it for a bigger bag filled full of
gold.[2]

[1] *Dialogue of Comfort*, Works, 1244.
[2] *Ibid.*, Works, 1250.

DESIRE OF DEATH.

Of him that is loth to leave this wretched world, mine heart is much in fear lest he die not well. Hard it is for him to be welcome that cometh against his will, that saith to God when he cometh to Him: "Welcome my Maker, maugre my teeth". But he that so loveth Him that he longeth to go to Him, my heart cannot give me but he shall be welcome, all were it so, that he should come ere he were well purged. For charity covereth a multitude of sins, and he that trusteth in God cannot be confounded. And Christ saith: "He that cometh to Me, I will not cast him out". And therefore let us never make our reckoning of long life; keep it while we may, because God hath so commanded, but if God give the occasion that with His good will we may go, let us be glad thereof and long to go to Him.[1]

[*In a letter to Dr. Wilson, More wrote as follows:—*]

I have, since I came to the Tower, looked once or twice to have given up the ghost ere this; and in good faith my heart waxed the lighter with hope thereof. Yet forget I not that I have a long reckoning and a great to give account of. But I put my trust in God, and in the merits of His bitter passion, and I beseech Him to give me and keep me the mind to look to be out of this world and to be with Him. For I can never but trust that whoso long to be with Him shall be welcome to Him; and, on the other side, my mind giveth me verily that any that ever shall come to Him shall full heartily wish to be with Him ere ever he shall come at Him.[2]

[1] *Dialogue of Comfort*, Works, 1168.

[2] Works, 1443. This was written in 1535, the year of More's martyrdom; but as far back as 1515 he had written in his *Utopia*: "Though they are compassionate to all that are sick, yet they lament

DESIRE OF HEAVEN.

Howbeit, if we would somewhat set less by the filthy voluptuous appetites of the flesh, and would by withdrawing from them, with help of prayer through the grace of God, draw nearer to the secret inward pleasure of the spirit, we should, by the little sipping that our hearts should have here now, and that sudden taste thereof, have such an estimation of the incomparable and uncogitable joy, that we shall have (if we will) in heaven by the very full draught thereof, whereof it is written : "I shall be satiate, satisfied, or fulfilled, when Thy glory, good Lord, shall appear," that is to wit, with the fruition of the sight of God's glorious majesty face to face ; that the desire, expectation, and heavenly hope thereof shall more encourage us, and make us strong to suffer and sustain for the love of God and salvation of our soul, than ever we could be moved to suffer here worldly pain by the terrible dread of all the horrible pains that damned wretches have in hell.

And, therefore, let us all that cannot now conceive such delight in the consideration of them as we should, have often in our eyes by reading, often in our ears by hearing, often in our mouths by rehearsing, often in our hearts

---

no man's death, except they see him loath to part with life. They think that such a man's appearance before God cannot be acceptable to Him, who, being called on, does not go out cheerfully, but is backward and unwilling, and is as it were dragged to it. They are struck with horror when they see any die in this manner, and carry them out in silence and with sorrow, and praying God that He would be merciful to the errors of the departed soul, they lay the body in the ground ; but when any die cheerfully and full of hope, they do not mourn for them, but sing hymns when they carry out their bodies, commending their souls very earnestly to God." (Burnet's translation.)

by meditation and thinking, those joyful words of Holy
Scripture, by which we learn how wonderful huge and great
those spiritual heavenly joys are of which our carnal hearts
have so feeble and so faint a feeling, and our dull worldly
wits so little able to conceive so much as a shadow of the
right imagination. A shadow I say: for as for the thing as
it is, that cannot only no fleshly carnal phantasy conceive,
but over that, no spiritual, ghostly person (peradventure)
neither, that here is living still in this world. For since the
very substance essential of all the celestial joys standeth in
blessed beholding of the glorious Godhead face to face,
there may no man presume or look to attain it in this life.[1]

APPEAL OF THE HOLY SOULS.

The comfort that we have here (in purgatory), except our
continual hope in our Lord God, cometh at seasons from
our Lady, with such glorious saints as either ourselves with
our own devotion while we lived, or ye with yours for us
since our decease and departing have made intercessors for
us. And, among others, right especially be we beholden to
the blessed spirits our own proper good angels; whom
when we behold coming with comfort to us, albeit that we
take great pleasure and greatly rejoice therein, yet it is not
without much confusion and shamefastness, to consider how
little we regarded our good angels, and how seldom we
thought upon them while we lived. They carry up your
prayers to God and good saints for us, and they bring down
from them the comfort and consolation to us, with which,
when they come and comfort us, only God and we know
what joy it is to our hearts and how heartily we pray for

[1] *Dialogue of Comfort*, Works, 1258-1259.

you. And, therefore, if God accept the prayer after His own favour borne towards him that prayeth, and the affection that he prayeth with, our prayer must needs be profitable : for we stand sure of His grace, and our prayer is for you so fervent, that ye can nowhere find any such affection upon earth.

And, therefore, since we lie so sore in pains, and have in our great necessity so great need of your help, and that ye may so well do it, whereby also shall rebound upon yourselves an inestimable profit, let never any slothful oblivion erase us out of your remembrance, or malicious enemy of ours cause you to be careless of us, or any greedy mind upon your goods withdraw your gracious alms from us. Think how soon ye shall come hither to us ; think what great grief and rebuke would then your unkindness be to you; what comfort, on the contrary part, when all we shall thank you, and what help ye shall have here of your goods sent hither.

Remember what kin ye and we be together ; what familiar friendship hath ere this been between us ; what sweet words ye have spoken, and what promise ye have made us. Let now your words appear, and your fair promise be kept. Now, dear friends, remember how nature and Christendom bindeth you to remember us. If any point of your old favour, any piece of your old love, any kindness of kindred, any care of acquaintance, any favour of old friendship, any spark of charity, any tender point of pity, any regard of nature, any respect of Christendom, be left in your breasts, let never the malice of a few fond fellows, a few pestilent persons borne towards the priesthood, religion and your Christian faith, erase out of your hearts the care of your kindred, all force of your old friends, and all remembrance of all Christian souls.

Remember our thirst while ye sit and drink, our hunger while ye be feasting, our restless watch while ye be sleeping, our sore and grievous pain while ye be playing, our hot, burning fire while ye be in pleasure and sporting. So mote God make your offspring after remember you ; so God keep you hence, or not long here, but bring you shortly to that bliss to which, for our Lord's love, help you to bring us, and we shall set hand to help you thither to us.[1]

EXILE.

Vincent.—Methinketh, Uncle, that captivity is a marvellous heavy thing, namely, when they shall, as they most commonly do, carry us far from home into a strange, uncouth land.

Antony.—I cannot say nay, but that some grief it is, Cousin, indeed. But yet as unto me not half so much as it would be, if they could carry me out into any such unknown country, that God could not wit where, nor find the mean how to come at me. But in good faith, Cousin, now, if my transmigration into a strange country should be any great grief unto me, the fault should be much in myself. For since I am very sure that whithersoever men convey me, God is no more verily here than He shall be there : if I get (as I may, if I will) the grace to set my whole heart on Him, and long for nothing but Him, it can then make no great matter to my mind, whether they carry me hence or leave me here. And then if I find my mind much offended therewith, that I am not still here in mine own

---

[1] *Supplication of Souls*, Works, 338.

country, I must consider that the cause of my grief is my
own wrong imagination, whereby I beguile myself with an
untrue persuasion, weening that this were mine own
country, whereas of truth it is not so. For as St. Paul
saith : " We have here no city nor dwelling country at all,
but we look for one that we shall come to ". And in what
country soever we walk in this world we be but as pilgrims
and wayfaring men. And if I should take any country for
my own, it must be that country to which I come, and not
the country from which I came. That country that shall be
to me then for a while so strange shall yet, pardie, be no
more strange to me, nor longer strange to me neither than
was mine own native country when I came first into it.[1]

This World a Prison.

And hereof it cometh, that by reason of this favour for a
time we wax, as I said, so wanton, that we forget where we
be ; weening that we were lords at large, whereas we be,
indeed (if we would well consider it), even silly, poor
wretches in prison. For, of truth, our very prison this
earth is : and yet thereof we cant us out (partly by
covenants that we make among us, and part by fraud, and
part by violence too) divers parts diversely to ourself, and
change the name thereof from the odious name of prison
and call it our own land and livelihood. Upon our prison
we build, our prison we garnish with gold, and make it
glorious. In this prison they buy and sell, in this prison
they brawl and chide, in this prison they run together and
fight ; in this they dice, in this they card, in this they pipe
and revel, in this they sing and dance. And in this prison

---

[1] *Dialogue of Comfort*, Works, 1237.

many a man reputed right honest letteth not for his
pleasure in the dark privily to play the knave. And thus
while God the king, and our chief jailor too, suffereth us
and letteth us alone, we ween ourself at liberty, and we
abhor the state of those whom we call prisoners, taking
ourselves for no prisoners at all.

In which false persuasion of wealth, and forgetfulness of
our own wretched state (which is but a wandering about for
a while in this prison of the world till we be brought unto
the execution of death), while we forget with our folly both
ourself and our jail, and our under-jailors, angels and devils
both, and our chief jailor God too—God that forgetteth not
us, but seeth us all the while well enough, and being sore
discontent to see so shrewd rule kept in the jail (besides
that He sendeth the hangman Death to put to execution
here and there, sometimes by the thousands at once), He
handleth many of the remnant, whose execution He for-
heareth yet unto a further time, even as hardly, and
punisheth them as sore in this common prison of the
world as there are any handled in those special prisons,
which for the hard handling used (you say) therein your
heart hath in such horror, and so sore abhorreth.[1]

PRISONERS.

[*Written in Prison.*]

In prison was Joseph while his brethren were at large,
and yet after were his brethren fain to seek upon him for
bread. In prison was Daniel, and the wild lions about him :
and yet even there God kept him harmless, and brought
him safe out again. If we think that He will not do the

[1] *Dialogue of Comfort*, Works, 1245.

like for us, let us not doubt but He will do for us either the like or better. For better may He do for us if He suffer us there to die.

St. John the Baptist was, ye wot well, in prison, while Herod and Herodias sat full merry at the feast, and the daughter of Herodias delighted them with her dancing, till with her dancing she danced off St. John's head. And now sitteth he with great feast in heaven at God's board, while Herod and Herodias full heavily sit in hell burning both twain, and to make them sport withal the devil with the damsel dance in the fire afore them. Finally, Cousin, to finish this piece with, our Saviour was Himself taken prisoner for our sake, and prisoner was He carried, and prisoner was He kept, and prisoner was He brought forth before Annas ; and prisoner from Annas carried unto Caiaphas. Then prisoner was He earried from Caiaphas unto Pilate, and prisoner was He sent from Pilate to King Herod : prisoner from Herod unto Pilate again. And so kept as prisoner to the end of His passion. The time of His imprisonment, I grant well, was not long ; but as for hard handling (which our hearts most abhor), He had as much in that short while as many men among them all in much longer time. And surely then, if we consider of what estate He was, and therewith that He was prisoner in such wise for our sake, we shall, I trow (but if we be worse than wretched beasts), never so shamefully play the unkind cowards as for fear of imprisonment sinfully to forsake Him ; nor so foolish neither as by forsaking of Him to give Him the occasion again to forsake us, and with the avoiding of an easier prison fall into a worse ; and, instead of a prison that cannot keep us long, fall into that prison out of which we can never come, whereas the short imprisonment would win us everlasting liberty.[1]

SHAME ENDURED FOR GOD.

Antony.—Now, if it so were, Cousin, that you should be brought through the broad high street of a great long city, and that all along the way that you were going there were on the one side of the way a rabble of ragged beggars and madmen that would despise you and dispraise you with all the shameful names that they could call you, and all the villanous words that they could say to you : and that there were then, along the other side of the same street where you should come by, a goodly company standing in a fair range, a row of wise and worshipful folk, allowing and commending you, more than fifteen times as many as that rabble of ragged beggars and railing madmen are. Would you let your way by your will, weening that you went unto your shame for the shameful jesting and railing of those mad, foolish wretches, or hold on your way with a good cheer and a glad heart, thinking yourself much honoured by the laud and approbation of that other honourable sort ?

Vincent.—Nay, by my troth, Uncle, there is no doubt, but I would much regard the commendation of those commendable folk, and not regard of a rush the railing of all those ribalds.

Antony.—Then, Cousin, can there no man that hath faith account himself shamed here by any manner death that he suffereth for the faith of Christ, while how vile and how shameful soever it seem in the sight here of a few worldly wretches, it is allowed and approved for very

[1] *Dialogue of Comfort*, Works, 1248.

6

precious and honourable in the sight of God and all the
glorious company of heaven, which as perfectly stand and
behold it, as those peevish people do, and are in number
more than an hundred to one : and of that hundred, every
one an hundred times more to be regarded and esteemed,
than of the other an hundred such whole rabbles. And
now, if a man would be so mad as, for fear of the rebuke
that he should have of such rebukeful beasts, he would be
ashamed to confess the faith of Christ : then with fleeing
from a shadow of shame he should fall into a very shame
and a deadly, painful shame indeed. For then hath our
Saviour made a sure promise, that He will show Himself
ashamed of that man before the Father of Heaven and all
His holy angels, saying : " He that is ashamed of Me and
My words, of him shall the Son of Man be ashamed when
He shall come in the majesty of Himself, and of His Father,
and of the holy angels ". And what manner a shameful
shame shall that be then ? If a man's cheeks glow sometimes for shame in this world, they will fall on fire for
shame when Christ shall show Himself ashamed of them
there.

To suffer the thing for Christ's faith, that we worldly,
wretched fools ween were villany and shame, the blessed
apostles reckoned for great glory. For they, when they
were with despite and shame scourged, and thereupon
commanded to speak no more of the name of Christ, went
their way from the council joyful and glad that God had
vouchsafed to do them the worship to suffer shameful despite
for the name of Jesu. And so proud were they of that
shame and villanous pain put unto them, that for all the
forbidding of that great council assembled they ceased not

every day to preach out the name of Jesu still, not in the Temple only, out of which they were fet and whipped for the same before, but also to double it with, went preaching that name about from house to house too.

I would, since we regard so greatly the estimation of worldly folk, we would, among many naughty things that they use, regard also some such as are good. For it is a manner among them in many places that some by handicraft, some by merchandise, some by other kind of living, rise and come forward in the world. And commonly folk are in youth set forth to convenient masters, under whom they be brought up and grow. But now, whensoever they find a servant such as disdaineth to do such things as he, that is his master, did while he was servant himself, that servant every man accounteth for a proud unthrift, never like to come to good proof. Let us, lo! mark and consider this, and weigh well therewithal, that our Master Christ, not the Master only, but the Maker too of all this whole world, was not so proud to disdain for our sakes the most villanous and most shameful death after the worldly account that then was used in the world, and the most despiteful mocking therewith, joined to most grievous pain, as crowning Him with sharp thorns that the blood ran down about His face: then they gave Him a reed in His hand for a sceptre, and kneeled down to Him, and saluted Him like a king in scorn, and beat then the reed upon the sharp thorns about His holy head. Now saith our Saviour, that the disciple or servant is not above his master. And, therefore, since our Master endured so many kinds of painful shame, very proud beasts may we well think ourselves if we disdain to do as our Master did : and whereas He through shame ascended

into glory, we would be so mad that we rather will fall into
everlasting shame, both before heaven and hell, than for fear
of a short worldly shame, to follow him into everlasting glory.[1]

A Patient Death.

"Then all His disciples departed from Him, and left
Him there alone." By this place, lo! may a man perceive
how hard and painful a thing the virtue of patience is.
For many men are there very well willing even stoutly to
die, how sure soever they be thereof, so they may give
stroke for stroke, and wound for wound, thereby to have
some part of their will fulfilled. But many, where all
comfort of revenging is gone, there to take death so
patiently as neither to strike again, not for a stripe to yield
so much as an angry word, this must I needs confess to be
so sovereign a point of patience, that as yet were not the
apostles themselves so strong as to be able to climb so
high. Who, having it fresh in their remembrance, how
boldly they had promised rather to be killed with Christ than
once to shrink from Him, did abide at the least wise so far
forth by the same, that if He would have licensed them to
fight and die manfully, they showed themselves all very
ready to have died for Him. Which thing Peter well
declared, too, in deed, by that he begun to practise upon
Malchus. But after that our Saviour would neither suffer
them again to fight nor to make any manner resistance,
then left they Him all alone, and fled away every one.[2]

Joy in Martyrdom.

Of this am I very sure, if we had the fifteenth part of the

[1] *Dialogue of Comfort*, Works, 1252.
[2] *Treatise on the Passion*, Works, 1399.

love to Christ that He both had, and bath unto us, all the
pain of this Turk's persecution could not keep us from
Him, but that there would be at this day as many martyrs
here in Hungary as have been afore in other countries
of old.

And of this point put I no doubt, but that if the Turk
stood even here, with all his whole army about him, and
every of them all were ready at our hand with all the
terrible torments that they could imagine, and (but if we
would forsake the faith) were setting their torments to us,
and to the increase of our terror, fell all at once in a shout,
with trumpets, tabrets, and tumbrels all blown up at once,
and all their guns let go therewith, to make us a fearful
noise; if there should suddenly then on the other side
the ground quake and rive atwain, and the devils rise out
of hell, and show themselves in such ugly shape as damned
wretches shall see them, and, with that hideous howling that
those hellhounds should screech, lay hell open on every
side round about our feet, that as we stood we should look
down into that pestilent pit, and see the swarm of souls in
the terrible torments there, we would wax so fraid of the
sight, that as for the Turk's host, we should scantly remember
we saw them. And in good faith for all that, yet think I
farther that if there might then appear the great glory of
God, the Trinity in His high marvellous majesty, our
Saviour in His glorious manhood, sitting on His throne with
His immaculate mother, and all that glorious company
calling us there unto them, and that yet our way should lie
through marvellous painful death before we could come at
them, upon the sight, I say, of that glory there would, I
ween, be no man that once would shrink thereat, but every

man would run on toward them in all that ever he might,
though there lay for malice to kill us by the way, both all
the Turk's tormentors, and all the devils too.

And, therefore, Cousin, let us well consider these things,
and let us have sure hope in the help of God, and then I
doubt not but that we shall be sure, that as the prophet
saith, the truth of His promise shall so compass us with a
pavice, that of this incursion of this midday devil, this
Turk's persecution, we shall never need to fear.   For either
if we trust in God well, and prepare us therefor, the Turk
shall never meddle with us, or else, if he do, harm shall he
none do us ; but, instead of harm, inestimable good.   Of
whose gracious help wherefore should we so sore now
despair, except we were so mad men as to ween that either
His power or His mercy were worn out already, when we see
so many a thousand holy martyrs by His holy help suffered
as much before, as any man shall be put to now ?   Or what
excuse can we have by the tenderness of our flesh, when we
can be no more tender than were many of them, among
whom were not only men of strength but also weak women
and children?   And since the strength of them all stood in
the help of God, and that the very strongest of them all was
never able of themselves, and with God's help the feeblest
of them all was strong enough to stand against all the
world, let us prepare ourselves with prayer, with our whole
trust in His help, without any trust in our own strength ; let
us think thereon and prepare us in our minds thereto long
before ; let us therein conform our will unto His, not
desiring to be brought unto the peril of persecution (for it
seemeth a proud, high mind to desire martyrdom), but
desiring help and strength of God, if He suffer us to come

to the stress, either being sought, found, or brought out against our wills, or else being by His commandment (for the comfort of our cure) bounden to abide.

Let us fall to fasting, to prayer, to almsdeed in time, and give that unto God that may be taken from us. If the devil put in our mind the saving of our land and our goods, let us remember that we cannot save them long. If he fear us with exile and fleeing from our country, let us remember that we be born into the broad world (and not like a tree to stick still in one place), and that whithersoever we go God shall go with us. If he threaten us with captivity, let us tell him again better is it to be thrall unto man a while for the pleasure of God, than by displeasing of God be perpetual thrall unto the devil. If he threat us with imprisonment, let us tell him we will rather be man's prisoners a while here on earth than by forsaking the faith be his prisoners for ever in hell. If he put in our minds the terror of the Turks, let us consider his false sleight therein ; for this tale he telleth us to make us forget him. But let us remember well, that in respect of himself the Turk is but a shadow, nor all that they all can do, can be but a fleabiting in comparison of the mischief that he goeth about. The Turks are but his tormentors, for himself doth the deed. Our Lord said in the Apocalypse : "The devil shall send some of you to prison to tempt you". He saith not that men shall, but that the devil shall himself. For, without question, the devil's own deed it is to bring us by his temptation with fear and force thereof into eternal damnation. And therefore saith St. Paul : " Our wrestling is not against flesh and blood, but against the princes and powers and ghostly enemies that be rulers of these

darknesses," etc. Thus may we see, that in such perse-
cutions it is the midday devil himself that maketh such
incursion upon us by the men that are his ministers, to
make us fall for fear. For till we fall, he can never hurt us.
And, therefore, saith St. James: "Stand against the devil,
and he shall flee from you". For he never runneth upon a
man to seize on him with his claws till he see him down on
the ground willingly fallen himself. For his fashion is to
set his servants against us, and by them to make us for fear
or for impatience to fall, and himself in the meanwhile
compasseth us, running and roaring like a ramping lion
about us, looking who will fall that he then may devour him.
"Your adversary, the devil," saith St. Peter, "like a
roaring lion, runneth about in circuit, seeking whom he
may devour." The devil it is, therefore, that (if we for fear
of men will fall) is ready to run upon us and devour us.
And is it wisdom, then, so much to think upon the Turks
that we forget the devil? What madman is he, that when
a lion were about to devour him, would vouchsafe to regard
the biting of a little foisting cur? Therefore, when he
roareth out upon us by the threats of mortal men, let us tell
him that with our inward eye we see him well enough, and
intend to stand and fight with him even hand to hand. If
he threaten us that we be too weak, let us tell him that our
captain Christ is with us, and that we shall fight with His
strength that hath vanquished him already, and let us fence
us with faith and comfort us with hope, and smite the devil
in the face with a firebrand of charity. For surely, if we
be of the tender, loving mind that our Master was, and not
hate them that kill us, but pity them and pray for them,
with sorrow for the peril that they work unto themselves; that

fire of charity thrown in his face striketh the devil suddenly so blind that he cannot see where to fasten a stroke on us.

When we feel us too bold, remember our own feebleness. When we feel us too faint, remember Christ's strength. In our fear, let us remember Christ's painful agony that Himself would (for our comfort) suffer before His passion, to the intent that no fear should make us despair. And ever call for His help, such as Himself list to send us, and then need we never to doubt but that either He shall keep us from the painful death, or shall not fail so to strength us in it that He shall joyously bring us to heaven by it. And then doth He much more for us than if He kept us from it. For as God did more for poor Lazar in helping him patiently to die for hunger at the rich man's door, than if He had brought him to the door all the rich glutton's dinner : so, though He be gracious to a man whom He delivereth out of painful trouble, yet doth He much more for a man if through right painful death He deliver him from this wretched world into eternal bliss.[1]

DEATH FOR CHRIST'S LOVE.

If we could, and would, with due compassion conceive in our minds a right imagination and remembrance of Christ's bitter, painful passion, of the many sore bloody strokes that the cruel tormentors, with rods and whips, gave Him upon every part of His holy, tender body, the scornful crown of sharp thorns beaten down upon His holy head, so straight and so deep, that on every part His blessed blood issued out and streamed down His lovely limbs,

[1] *Dialogue of Comfort*, Works, 1261.

drawn and stretched out upon the cross, to the intolerable
pain of His forbeaten and sore beaten veins and sinews,
new feeling with the cruel stretching and straining
pain, far passing any cramp in every part of His
blessed body at once : then the great long nails
cruelly driven with hammers through His holy hands and
feet, and in this horrible pain lift up and let hang with the
poise of all His body bearing down upon the painful
wounded places, so grievously pierced with nails, and in
such torment (without pity, but not without.many despites)
suffered to be pined and pained the space of more than
three long hours, till Himself willingly gave up unto His
Father His holy soul : after which, yet to show the
mightiness of their malice, after His holy soul departed,
they pierced His holy heart with a sharp spear, at which
issued out the holy blood and water whereof His holy
sacraments have inestimable secret strength : if we would,
I say, remember these things, I verily suppose that the
consideration of His incomparable kindness could not fail
in such wise to inflame our key-cold hearts, and set them
on fire in His love, that we should find ourselves not only
content, but also glad and desirous, to suffer death for His
sake, that so marvellous lovingly letted not to sustain so
far passing painful death for ours.

Would God we would here to the shame of our cold
affection again towards God, for such fervent love and
inestimable kindness of God towards us : would God we
would, I say, but consider what hot affection many of these
fleshly lovers have borne, and daily do bear to those upon
whom they doat ! How many of them have not letted to
jeopard their lives, and how many have willingly lost their

lives indeed without either great kindness showed them
before (and afterward, you wot well, they could nothing
win), but even that it contented and satisfied their mind,
that by their death their lover should clearly see how
faithfully they loved ? The delight whereof imprinted in
their phantasy not assuaged only, but counterpoised also
(they thought) all their pain. Of these affections with the
wonderful dolorous effects following thereon, not only old
written stories, but over that I think in every country
Christian and heathen both, experience giveth us proof
enough. And is it not then a wonderful shame for us for
the dread of temporal death to forsake our Saviour that
willingly suffered so painful death rather than He would
forsake us, considering that beside that He shall for our
suffering so highly reward us with everlasting wealth ? Oh !
if he that is content to die for her love, of whom he looketh
after for no reward, and yet by his death goeth from her,
might by his death be sure to come to her, and ever after
in delight and pleasure to dwell with her : such a lover
would not let here to die for her twice. And how cold
ꞁlovers be we then unto God, if rather than die for Him
once we will refuse Him and forsake Him for ever that both
died for us before, and bath also provided that if we die
here for Him we shall in heaven everlastingly both live and
also reign with Him. For, as St. Paul saith, if we suffer
with Him we shall reign with Him.

How many Romans, how many noble courages of other
sundry countries have willingly given their own lives, and
suffered great deadly pains, and very painful deaths for their
countries, and the respect of winning by their deaths the
only reward of worldly renown and fame ! And should we

then shrink to suffer as much for eternal honour in heaven and everlasting glory ? The devil hath also some so obstinate heretics that endure wittingly painful death for vain glory : and is it not more than shame, that Christ shall see His Catholics forsake His faith rather than suffer the same for heaven and very glory ? Would God, as I many times have said, that the remembrance of Christ's kindness in suffering His passion for us, the consideration of hell that we should fall in by forsaking of Him, the joyful meditation of eternal life in heaven, that we shall win with this short, temporal death patiently taken for Him, had so deep a place in our breast as reason would they should, and as (if we would do our devoir towards it, and labour for it, and pray therefor) I verily think they should. For then, should they so take up our mind, and ravish it all another way, that as a man hurt in a fray feeleth not some-time his wound, nor yet is not ware thereof till his mind fall more thereon, so farforth, that sometime another man showeth him that he hast lost a hand before he perceive it himself. So the mind ravished in the thinking deeply of those other things, Christ's death, hell, and heaven, were likely to minish and put away of our painful death four parts of the feeling, either of the fear or of the pain.[1]

MEDITATIONS AND PRAYERS COMPOSED IN THE TOWER.

Give me Thy grace, good Lord, to set the world at naught ; to set my mind fast upon Thee ; and not to hang upon the blast of men's mouths.

To be content to be solitary ; not to long for worldly company ; little and little utterly to cast off the world, and rid

---

[1] *Dialogue of Comfort*, Works, 1260.

my mind of all the business thereof; not to long to hear
of any worldly things, but that the hearing of worldly
phantasies may be to me displeasant.

Gladly to be thinking of God; piteously to call for His
help; to lean unto the comfort of God; busily to labour to
love Him.

To know mine own vility and wretchedness; to humble
and meeken myself under the mighty hand of God. To
bewail my sins past; for the purging of them patiently to
suffer adversity; gladly to bear my purgatory here; to be
joyful of tribulations; to walk the narrow way that leadeth
to life.

To bear the cross with Christ; to have the last things in
remembrance; to have ever afore mine eye my death that is
ever at hand; to make death no stranger to me; to foresee
and consider the everlasting fire of hell; to pray for pardon
before the Judge come.

To have continually in mind that passion that Christ
suffered for me; for His benefits uncessantly to give Him
thanks.

To buy the time again, that I before have lost; to abstain
from vam confabulations; to eschew light, foolish mirth;
and gladness; recreations not necessary to cut off; of worldly
substance, friends, liberty, life, and all, to set the loss at
right naught for the winning of Christ.

To think my most enemies my best friends; for the
brethren of Joseph could never have done him so much
good with their love and favour as they did him with their
malice and hatred.

These minds are more to be desired of every man than
all the treasure of all the princes and kings, Christian and

heathen, were it gathered and laid together all upon one heap.

PRAYER.

[Composed after being condemned to death.]

PATER NOSTER. AVE MARIA. CREDO.

O Holy Trinity, the Father, the Son, and the Holy Ghost, three equal and coeternal Persons and one Almighty God, have mercy on me, vile, abject, abominable, sinful wretch, meekly knowledging before Thine High Majesty my long-continued sinful life, even from my very childhood hitherto.

In my childhood (*in this point and that point*). After my childhood (*in this point and that point, and so forth by every age*).

Now, good gracious Lord, as Thou givest me Thy grace to knowledge them, so give me Thy grace not only in word but in heart also, with very sorrowful contrition to repent them and utterly to forsake them. And forgive me those sins also in which, by mine own default, through evil affections and evil custom, my reason is with sensuality so blinded that I cannot discern them for sin. And illumine, good Lord, mine heart, and give me Thy grace to know them and to knowledge them, and forgive me my sins negligently forgotten, and bring them to my mind with grace to be purely confessed of them.

Glorious God, give me from henceforth Thy grace, with little respect unto the world, so to set and fix firmly mine heart upon Thee, that I may say with Thy blessed apostle St. Paul : " Mundus mihi crucifixus est et ego mundo. Mihi vivere Christus est et mori lucrum. Cupio dissolvi et esse cum Christo."

Give me Thy grace to amend my life and to have an eye to mine end without grudge of death, which to them that die in Thee, good Lord, in the gate of a wealthy life.

Almighty God, Doce me facere voluntatem Tuam. Fac me currere in odore unguentorum tuorum. Apprehende manum meam dexteram et deduc me in via recta propter inimicos meos. Trahe me post te. In chamo et freno maxillas meas constringe, quum non approximo ad te.

O glorious God, all sinful fear, all sinful sorrow and pensiveness, all sinful hope, all sinful mirth and gladness take from me. And on the other side, concerning such fear, such sorrow, such heaviness, such comfort, consolation, and gladness as shall be profitable for my soul: Fac mecum secundum magnam bonitatem tuam Domine.

Good Lord, give me the grace, in all my fear and agony, to have recourse to that great fear and wonderful agony that Thou, my sweet Saviour, hadst at the Mount of Olivet before Thy most bitter passion, and in the meditation thereof to conceive ghostly comfort and consolation profitable for my soul.

Almighty God, take from me all vain-glorious minds, all appetites of mine own praise, all envy, covetise, gluttony, sloth, and lechery, all wrathful affections, all appetite of revenging, all desire or delight of other folk's harm, all pleasure in provoking any person to wrath and anger, all delight of exprobation or insultation against any person in their affliction and calamity.

And give me, good Lord, an humble, lowly, quiet, peaceable, patient, charitable, kind, tender, and pitiful mind with all my works, and all my words, and all my thoughts, to have a taste of Thy holy, blessed Spirit.

Give me, good Lord, a full faith, a firm hope, and a

fervent charity, a love to the good Lord incomparable above the love to myself; and that I love nothing to Thy displeasure, but everything in an order to Thee.

Give me, good Lord, a longing to be with Thee, not for the avoiding of the calamities of this wretched world, nor so much for the avoiding of the pains of purgatory, nor of the pains of hell neither, nor so much for the attaining of the joys of heaven in respect of mine own commodity, as even for a very love to Thee.

And bear me, good Lord, Thy love and favour, which thing my love to Thee-ward, were it never so great, could not, but of Thy great goodness deserve.

And pardon me, good Lord, that I am so bold to ask so high petitions, being so vile a sinful wretch, and so unworthy to attain the lowest. But yet, good Lord, such they be as I am bounden to wish, and should be nearer the effectual desire of them if my manifold sins were not the let. From which, O glorious Trinity, vouchsafe, of Thy goodness to wash me with that blessed blood that issued out of Thy tender body, O sweet Saviour Christ, in the divers torments of Thy most bitter passion.

Take from me, good Lord, this lukewarm fashion, or rather key-cold manner of meditation, and this dulness in praying unto Thee. And give me warmth, delight, and quickness in thinking upon Thee. And give me Thy grace to long for Thine holy sacraments, and specially to rejoice in the presence of Thy very blessed body, sweet Saviour Christ, in the holy sacrament of the altar, and duly to thank Thee for Thy gracious visitation therewith, and at that high memorial with tender compassion to remember and consider Thy most bitter passion.

Make us all, good Lord, virtually participant of that holy sacrament this day, and every day. Make us all lively members, sweet Saviour Christ, of Thine holy mystical body, Thy Catholic Church.

Dignare, Domine, die isto sine peccato nos custodire. Miserere nostri, Domine, miserere nostri.

Fiat misericordia tua, Domine, super nos, quemadmodum speravimus in te.

In te, Domine, speravi, non confundar in æternum.

R. Ora pro nobis, sancta Dei genitrix.

V. Ut digni efficiamur promissionibus Christi.

Pro amicis.

Almighty God, have mercy on N. and N. (*with special meditation and consideration of every friend, as godly affections and occasion requireth*).

Pro inimicis.

Almighty God, have mercy on N. and N., and on all that bear me evil will, and would me harm, and their faults and mine together by such easy, tender, merciful means as Thine infinite wisdom best can devise, vouchsafe to amend and redress and make us saved souls in heaven together, where we may ever live and love together with Thee and Thy blessed saints, O glorious Trinity, for the bitter passion of our sweet Saviour Christ. Amen.

God, give me patience in tribulation and grace in everything, to conform my will to Thine, that I may truly say : " Fiat voluntas tua, sieut in cœlo et in terra ".

The things, good Lord, that I pray for, give me Thy grace to labour for. Amen.[1]

---

[1] Works, 1416.

PART THE SECOND.

DOGMATIC.

DOGMATIC.

FAITH AND REASON.

I cannot see why ye should reckon reason for an enemy to faith,[1] except ye reckon every man for your enemy that is your better and hurteth you not. Then were one of your five wits enemy to another; and our feeling should abhor our sight because we may see further by four mile than we may feel. . . . I pray you that our Lord was born of a virgin how know you ? " Marry (quoth he) by Scripture." " How know you (quoth I), that ye should believe the Scripture ?" " Marry (quoth he) by faith." " Why (quoth I), what doth faith tell you therein ? " " Faith (quoth he) telleth me that Holy Scripture is things of truth written by the secret teaching of God." " And whereby know you (quoth I) that ye should believe God ?" " Whereby ? (quoth he) this is a strange question. Every man may well weet that." " That is truth (quoth I) ; but is there any horse or any ass that wotteth that ? " " None (quoth he) that I wot of, but if Balaam's ass anything understood thereof, for he spake like a good reasonable ass." " If no brute beast can wit that (quoth I) and every man may, what is the cause why man may and other beasts may not ? " " Marry (quoth he), for man hath reason and they have none." " Ah ! well

[1] Luther and the early Protestants constantly denounced reason and philosophy.

then (quoth I), reason must he needs have then that shall
perceive what he should believe. And so must reason
not resist faith, but walk with her, and as her handmaid
so wait upon her that, as contrary as ye take her, yet of a
truth faith goeth never without her.

"But likewise, as if a maid be suffered to run on the
bridle, or to be cup-shotten,[1] or wax too proud, she will
then wax copious and chop logic with her mistress, and
fare sometimes as if she were frantic ; so if reason be
suffered to run out at riot, and wax over-high hearted and
proud, she will not fail to fall in rebellion towards her
mistress faith. But on the other side, if she be well,
brought up and well guided and kept in good temper, she
shall never disobey faith, being in her right mind."[2]

Heathen Philosophy.

[The old heathen moral philosophers.]

They never stretch so far but that they leave untouched,
for lack of necessary knowledge, that special point which is
not only the chief comfort of all, but without which also, all
other comforts are nothing : that is, to wit, the referring of
the final end of their comfort unto God, and to repute and
take for the special cause of comfort, that by the patient
sufferance of their tribulation they shall attain His favour,
and for their pain receive reward at His hand in heaven.
And for lack of knowledge of this end they did (as they
needs must) leave untouched also the very special mean,
without which we can never attain to this comfort ; that is,
to wit, the gracious aid and help of God to move, stir, and
guide us forward in the referring all our ghostly comfort,

---

[1] Tipsy.   [2] *Dialogue of Comfort*, Works, 153.

yea and our worldly comfort too, all unto that heavenly
end. And therefore, as I say, for the lack of these things,
all their comfortable counsels are very far insufficient.
Howbeit, though they be far unable to cure our disease of
themselves, and therefore are not sufficient to be taken for
our physicians, some good drugs have they yet in their
shops, for which they may be suffered to dwell among our
apothecaries if their medicines be not made of their own
brains, but after the bills made by the great physician God,
prescribing the medicines Himself and correcting the faults
of their erroneous recipes. For without this way taken
with them they shall not fail to do, as many bold blind
apothecaries do, who either for lucre or of a foolish pride,
give sick folk medicines of their own devising ; and therewith kill up in corners many such simple folk, as they find
so foolish to put their lives in such lewd and unlearned
blind bayards' hands.[1]

We shall, therefore, neither fully receive these philosophers' reasons in this matter nor yet utterly refuse them ;
but using them in such order as shall beseem them, the
principal and the effectual medicines against these diseases
of tribulation shall we fetch from that high, great and
excellent Physician, without whom we could never be
healed of our very deadly disease of damnation.[2]

The Known Catholic Church.

Since it is agreed between us, and granted through
Christendom, and a conclusion very true, that by the

---

[1] A bayard is properly a bay horse; but a blind bayard was a
common expression for a rash, headstrong man.

[2] *Dialogue of Comfort*, Works, 1142.

Church we know the Scripture:[1] Which Church is that by which we know the Scripture? Is it not this company and congregation of all these nations that, without factions taken and precision from the remnant, profess the name and faith of Christ? By this Church know we the Scripture and this is that very Church, and this hath begun at Christ, and hath had Him for their head, and St. Peter His vicar after Him the head under Him, and always since the successors of Him continually, and have had His holy faith and His blessed sacraments and His holy Scriptures delivered, kept, and conserved therein by God and His holy Spirit.

And albeit, some nations fall away, yet likewise as how many boughs so ever fall from the tree, though they fall more than be left thereon, yet they make no doubt which is the very tree, although each of them were planted again in another place, and grew to a greater than the stock he came first of; right so, while we see and well know that all the companies and sects of heretics and schismatics, how great so ever they grow, came out of this Church that I speak of, we know evermore that the heretics be they that be severed, and the Church the stock that they all came out of.[2]

God's Perpetual Apostle.

In such things as God seeth most need, and the hereties most busy to assault His Church, there doth He most specially fence in His Church with miracles. As in the reverence of images, relics, and pilgrimages, and worshipping of saints and His holy sacraments, and most of all that holy sacrament of the altar, His own blessed body; for which

[1] Luther had conceded thus much.
[2] *Dialogue of Comfort*, Works, 185.

manner of things He hath wrought and daily doth many wonderful miracles, and the like of those that He wrought in the time of His apostles, to show and make proof that *His Catholic Church is His perpetual Apostle*, how many nations so ever fall therefrom, and how little and small so ever it be left.[1]

THE PILLAR AND GROUND OF THE TRUTH.

"The Church," saith St. Paul, "is the pillar and ground of the truth." This word "the pillar," and this word "the ground," or the foot of the pillar, do not barely signify strength in the standing by themselves, but they signify therewith the bearing up of some other things, and that they be sure things for some other things to rest and lean upon. As the roof of a church is borne up from ruin and falling by the pillars upon which it resteth, so is the Church the pillar or the foot or ground of truth upon whose doctrine every man may rest and stand sure. Now if the very Church which cannot err be a congregation invisible and a company unknown, though every one of them have the very truth in himself, yet if I cannot know that Church I cannot lean to that Church as to a sure pillar of truth.[2]

THE HOLY SEE INFALLIBLE.

But now, whoso look upon these two laws shall soon see that the cause why he (Barns) did not (quote them fully and give accurate references) was because he durst not. For the law *xxiv. que i A recta* speaketh clear against him. For that law saith nothing else but that the very true faith without error hath been ever preserved in the See Apostolic,

---

[1] *Conf. of Tindale*, Works, 458.   [2] *Ibid.*, Works, 742.

and as the law calleth it there, the mother of all Churches, the Church of Rome. And therefore this law (ye see well) was not for his purpose to bring in, but instead of the law he layeth us forth a patch of the gloss.[1]

THE DECRETALS.

These words which Tindale saith are a plain law made by the Pope, are indeed incorporate in the book of the Decrees in the same distinction and place where Tindale allegeth them. But there is Tindale very ignorant if he know not that though there be in the book of the Decrees many things that be laws, and that were by divers Popes and divers synods and councils made for laws, yet are there in that book many things beside that neither were made by any synod nor by any Pope, but written by divers good holy men, out of whose holy works as well as out of synods and councils and Popes' writing, Gratian, a good, virtuous, and well-learned man, compiled and gathered that book, which is therefore called the Decrees of Gratian.

Now is everything that is alleged and inserted of such authority there as it is in the place out of which Gratian gathered it. Now the words which Tindale bringeth forth be not the words of any Pope, but they be the words of the blessed martyr St. Boniface. Wherein Tindale plainly showeth his plain, open falsehood, except he were so wise that he had weened the Pope had made it for a law because it beginneth with *Si Papa*, like him that because he read in the mass book *Te igitur clementissime pater*, preached unto the parish that *Te igitur* was St. Clement's father.[2]

GENERAL COUNCILS.

Now think I, that though Friar Barns will not believe any

---

[1] *Conf. of Tindale*, Works, 776.   [2] *Ibid.*, Works, 623.

general council, but if the whole Church be there, yet he looketh not that in any council everything should stay and nothing pass, till all the whole assembly were agreed so fully upon one side that there were not so much as any one man there of the contrary mind. For though some one might in some one matter be of a better mind at the first than the multitude, yet in a council of wise men when it were proposed it were likely to be perceived and allowed. And in a council of Christian men the Spirit of God inclineth every good man to declare his mind, and inclineth the congregation to consent and agree upon that that shall be the best, either precisely the best, or the best at the least wise for the season. Which, when so ever it shall be better at any other time to change, the same Spirit of God inclineth His Church either at a new council, or by as full and whole consent as any council can have, to abrogate the first and turn it into the better.

But when the council and the congregation agreeth and consenteth upon a point, if a few wilful folk, far the less both in number, wit, learning and honest living, would so claim and say that themselves would not agree, yet were their forwardness no let unto the determination or to the making of the law, but that it might stand till it be by another like authority changed.

But these changes that I speak of, I mean in things to be done, and not in truths to be believed. For in divers times divers things may be convenient, and divers manners of doing. But in matters of belief and faith, which be truths revealed and declared by God unto man, though that in divers times there may be more things farther and farther revealed, and other than were declared at the first, yet can there never anything be by God revealed after, that can be contrary to anything revealed by Himself before.[1]

THE CHURCH DISPERSED.

Now shall I further say, that whatsoever all Christian people would determine if they came to one assembly together; look what strength it should have if they so did, the same strength hath it, if they be all of the same mind, though they make no decree thereof, nor come not together therefor.   For when all Christian people be by the same Spirit of God brought into a full agreement and consent that the vow of chastity may not be, by his pleasure that made it, broken and set at naught, but that whoso doth break it committeth a horrible sin, and that whoso holdeth the contrary of this is a heretic, then is this belief as sure a truth as though they had—all the whole company-- come to a council together to determine it.[2]

HERETICS.

Heretics be all they that obstinately hold any self-minded opinion contrary to the doctrine that the common known Catholic Church teacheth and holdeth for necessary to salvation.[3]

DEVELOPMENT OF DOCTRINE.

If he will say that sometimes the doctors which we call holy saints have not all agreed in one, but some hath sometimes thought in some one thing otherwise than others have done, then his saying is nothing to the purpose.   For God doth reveal His truths not always in one manner, but sometimes He showeth it out at once, as He will have it known, and men bound

---

[1] *Conf. of Tindale*, Works, 778.   [2] *Ibid.*, Works, 788.
[3] *Debel. of Salem and Bizance*, Works, 941.

forthwith to believe it, as He showed Moses what he would have Pharao do. Sometimes He showeth it leisurely, suffering His flock to commune and dispute thereon, and in their treating of the matter suffereth them with good mind, and Scripture, and natural wisdom, with invocation of His spiritual help, to search and seek for the truth, and to vary for the while in their opinions, till that He reward their virtuous diligence with leading them secretly into the consent and concord, and belief of the truth by His Holy Spirit, *qui facit unanimes in domo* (Ps. lxvii. 7), "which maketh His flock in one mind in His House, that is, to wit, His Church". So that in the meantime the variance is without sin, and maketh nothing against the evidence of the Church, except Tindale will say that he will neither believe St. Peter nor St. Paul in anything that they teach, because that once they varied in the manner of their doctrine, as appeareth (Gal. ii. 11-14).[1]

EVANGELICALS.

It is now, and some years already past hath been, the name (viz., Evangelicals) by which they have been as commonly called in all the countries Catholic as by their own very name of heretic. And the occasion thereof grew first of that, that themselves took the name Evangelical arrogantly to themselves, both by their evangelical liberty that they pretended, as folk that would live under the Gospel and under no man's law beside, and because they would also believe nothing farther than the very Scriptures, all which they take now under the name of the Gospel. Now, when they had taken this name commonly upon themselves, the Catholics, telling them that they neither lived nor believed according to

[1] *Conf. of Tindale*, Works, 456.

the Gospel, listed not yet to call them by the same name too, and that not to their praise, but to their rebuke—in such manner of speaking as every man useth when he calleth one self [same] naughty lad, both a "shrewd boy" and a "good son," the one in the proper simple speech, the other by the figure of irony or antiphrasis.[1]

WHAT MORE THOUGHT OF LUTHERANISM.

Surely there was never sect of heretics yet that there was so great madness to believe as these. For of other heretics that have been of old, every sect had some one heresy, or else very few. Now these heretics came in with almost all that ever they held, and yet more, too. All the other heretics had some pretext of holiness in their living; these shameless heretics live in open, shameless, incestuous lechery, and call it matrimony. The old heretics did stick upon Scripture when it was yet in a manner new received, and they contended upon the understanding at such time as there had few Christian writers expounded the Scripture before them ; so as they might the better say to the Catholic Church: "Why may not we perceive the Scripture as well as you?" But these new heretics be so far from shame, that in the understanding of Scripture, and in the affirming of all their heresies, they would be believed by their only word against all the old holy doctors that have been since the death of Christ unto this day, and that in those rotten heresies, too, which they find condemned to the devil by the general councils of all Christendom a thousand years before their days.

And most mad of all in denying the sacraments which

---

[1] *Debel. of Salem and Bizance*, Works, 939.

they find received and believed, used and honoured so dearly from the beginning, that never was there heretic that durst for very shame so boldly bark against them, till that now in these latter days the devil hath broken his chains, and of all extreme abomination hath set his poisoned barrel abroach, from the dreggy draught whereof God keep every good Christian man, and such as have drunken thereof give them grace to vomit it out again betime.[1]

RESULTS OF LUTHERANISM (A.D. 1528).

Of all the heretics that ever sprang in Christ's Church, the very worst and the most beastly be these Lutherans, as their opinions and their lewd living showeth. And let us never doubt but all that be of that sect, if any seem good, as very few do, yet will they in conclusion decline to the like lewd living as their master and their fellows do, if they might once (as by God's grace they never shall) frame the people to their own frantic fantasy. Which dissolute living they be driven to dissemble, because their audience is not yet brought to the point to hear, which they surely trust to bring about, and to frame this realm after the fashion of Switzerland or Saxony, or some other parts of Germany, where their sect hath already fordone the faith, pulled down the churches, polluted the temples, put out and despoiled all good religious folk, joined friars and nuns together in lechery, despited all saints, blasphemed our Blessed Lady, cast down Christ's Cross, thrown out the Blessed Sacrament, refused all good laws, abhorred all good governance, rebelled against all rulers, fallen to fight among themselves, and so many thousand slain, that the land lieth in many

---

[1] *Conf. of Tindale*, Works, 394.

places in manner desert and desolate. And finally, that most abominable is of all, of all their own ungracious deeds they lay the fault on God, taking away the liberty of man's will, ascribing all our deeds to destiny, with all reward or punishment pursuing upon all our doings; whereby they take away all diligence and good endeavour to virtue, all withstanding and striving against vice, all care of heaven, all fear of hell, all cause of prayer, all desire of devotion, all exhortation to good, all dehortation from evil, all praise of well-doing, all rebuke of sin, all the laws of the world, all reason among men, set all wretchedness abroach, no man at liberty, and yet every man do what he will, calling it not his will, but his destiny, laying their sin to God's ordinance and their punishment to God's cruelty, and, finally, turning the nature of man into worse than a beast, and the goodness of God into worse than a devil. And all this good fruit would a few mischievous persons, some for desire of a large liberty to an unbridled lewdness, and some of a high devilish pride cloaked under pretext of good zeal and simpleness, undoubtedly bring into this realm, if the prince and prelates and the good faithful people did not in the beginning meet with their malice.[1]

LUTHER A REFORMER.

Tindale.—Though our popish hypocrites succeed Christ and His Apostles, and have their Scripture, yet they be fallen from the faith and living of them, and are heretics, and had need of a John Baptist to convert them.

More.—If Tindale will have Luther taken now for a new St. John, as of the old St. John it was of old prophesied

---

[1] *Dialogue of Comfort*, Works, 284.

by the mouth of Esay that he should be the voice of one crying in desert: "Make ready the way of our Lord, make straight the paths of our God in wilderness"; so must Tindale now tell us by what old prophet God hath prophesied that He would in the latter days, when the faith were sore decayed, and charity greatly cooled, rear up a friar that should wed a nun, and from a harlot's bed step up into the pulpit and preach. For, but if he prove his authority the better, either by prophecy or by marvellous miracle, it will be long of likelihood ere ever any wise man ween that God would ever send any such abominable beast, to turn the world to the right way, and make a perfect people.[1]

DOGS AND HOGS.

Tindale.—Howbeit there be swine that receive no learning, but to defile it, and there be dogs that rend all good learning with their teeth.

More.—If there be such swine and such dogs. as indeed there be, as our Saviour Himself witnesseth in the Gospel, then is it false that Tindale told us before that all standeth in teaching. Then to keep such from doing harm, we must not only teach and preach, we must yoke them from breaking hedges, and ring them from rooting, and have bandogs to drive them out of the corn, and lead them out by the ears.

And if there be such dogs, what availeth to teach them that will not learn, but rend all good learning with their teeth? And, therefore, to such dogs men may not only preach, but must, with whips and bats, beat them well, and keep them from tearing of good learning with their dogs' teeth, yea, and from barking both, and chastise them,

---

[1] *Conf. of Tindale,* Works, 650.

and make them couch, quail, till they lie still and hearken what is said unto them. And by such means be both swine kept from doing harm, and dogs fall sometimes so well to learning that they can stand upon their hinder feet, and hold their hands afore them prettily like a maid, yea, and learn to dance, too, after their master's pipe. Such an effectual thing is punishment, whereas bare teaching will not suffice.[1]

St. Thomas Aquinas.

Now where the wretch (Tindale) raileth by name upon that holy doctor, St. Thomas, a man of that learning that the great excellent wits and the most cunning men that the Church of Christ hath had since his days, have esteemed and called him the very flower of theology ; and a man of that true perfect faith and Christian living thereto, that God hath Himself testified His Holiness by many a great miracle, and made him honoured here in His Church in earth, as He hath exalted him to great glory in heaven ;— this glorious saint of God doth this devilish, drunken soul abominably blaspheme, and calleth him liar and falsifier of Scripture, and maketh him no better than "draff". But this drowsy drudge hath drunken so deep in the devil's dregs, that, but if he wake and repent himself the sooner, he may hap, ere aught long, to fall into the mashing-vat, and turn himself into draf, as the hogs of hell shall feed upon and fill their bellies thereof.[2]

[1] *Conf. of Tindale*, Works, 586.

[2] *Ibid.*, Works, 679. The last sentence of this passage is quoted by some admirers of Tindale to show the length and depth of ribaldry to which Sir Thomas More went. The passage shows the intense indignation stirred up in Sir Thomas by the ribaldries and blasphemies of Tindale against St. Thomas and the other doctors of the Church.

THE CHURCH'S LAWS.

More.—Our Saviour said that the scribes and the phari-sees, besides the law of Moses, on whose seat they sat, did lay great fardels, and fast bound them on other men's backs, to the bearing whereof they would not move a finger themselves. And yet for all that He bade the people do what their prelates would bid them, though the burden were heavy, and let not to do it, though they should see the bidders do clean contrary—for which He added : "But as they do, do not you ".

Messenger.—By our Lady, I like not this glose. For it maketh all for the bonds, by which the laws of the Church bind us to more ado than the Jews were almost with Moses' law. And I wot well Christ said : " Come to Me ye that be overcharged, and I shall refresh you ". And His apostles said that the bare law of Moses, besides[1] the ceremonies that were set to by the scribes and pharisees, were more than ever they were able to bear and fulfil. And, therefore, Christ came to call us into a law of liberty, and that was in taking away the band of those very ceremonial laws. And, therefore, saith our Saviour of the law that He called us unto : " My yoke, saith He, is fit and easy, and My burden but light ". Whereby it appeareth He meant to take away the strait yoke and put on a more easy, and to take off the heavy burden and lay on a lighter. Which He had not done if He would lade us with a fardel full of men's laws, more than a cart can carry away.

More.—The laws of Christ be made by Himself and His holy Spirit for the government of His people, and be not in

[1] *i.e.,* apart from.

hardness and difficulty of keeping anything like to the laws of Moses. And thereof durst I for need make yourself judge. For if ye bethink you well, I ween, if it were at this age now to chose, you would rather be bound to many of the laws of Christ's Church than to the circumcision alone.

Nor to as much ease as we ween that Christ called us, yet be not the laws that have been made by His Church of half the pain nor half the difficulty that His own be, which Himself putteth in the Gospel, though we set aside the counsels. It is, I trow, more hard not to swear at all than not to forswear, to forbear each angry word than not to kill; continual watch and prayer than a few days appointed. Then what an anxiety and solicitude is there in the forbearing of every idle word! What a hard threat, after the worldly compt, for a small matter! Never was there almost so sore a word said unto the Jews by Moses as is to us by Christ in that word alone, where He saith that we shall of every idle word give accompt at the day of judgment.

What say ye then by divorces restrained, the liberty of divers wives withdrawn, where they had liberty to wed for their pleasure if they cast a fantasy to any that they took in the war?

Messenger.—One of that ware is enough to make any one man war.

More.—Now that is merrily said; but though one eye were enough for a fletcher, yet is he for store content to keep twain, and would, though they were sometime sore both and should put him to some pain. What ease also call you this, that we be bound to abide all sorrow and shameful death and all martyrdom upon pain of perpetual damnation for the profession of our faith? Trow ye that these easy words of His easy yoke and light burden were not as well spoken to His apostles as to you; and yet, what ease called He them to? Called He not them to watching, fasting, praying, preaching, walking, hunger, thirst, cold and heat, beating, scourging, prisonment, painful and shameful death? The ease of His yoke standeth not in bodily ease, nor the lightness of His burden standeth not in the slackness of any bodily pain, except we be so wanton that where Himself had not heaven without pain we look to come thither with play; but it standeth in the sweetness of hope, whereby we feel in our pain a pleasant taste of heaven. This is the thing, as holy St. Gregory Nazianzen declareth, that refresheth men that are laden and maketh our yoke easy and our burden light; not any delivering from the laws of the Church, or from any good temporal laws either, into a lewd liberty of slothful rest. For that were not an easy yoke, but a pulling of the head out of the yoke. Nor it were not a light burden, but all the burden discharged, contrary to the words of St. Paul and St. Peter both, which as well understood the words of their Master as these men do; and as a thing consonant and well agreeable therewith do command us obedience to our superiors and rulers, one and other, in things by God not forbidden, although they be hard and sore.[1]

Penance.

Tindale here beareth us in hand that the Scripture speaketh not of penance, because himself giveth the Greek word ($\mu\epsilon\tau\alpha\nu\omicron\iota\alpha$) another English name. And because that

---

[1] *Dialogue of Comfort*, Works, 142.

Tindale calleth it forethinking and repentance, therefore all Englishmen have ever hitherto misused their own language in calling the thing by the name of penance. Now, as for the word penance, whatsoever the Greek word be, it ever was, and yet is lawful enough (so that Tindale give us leave) to call anything in English by what word soever Englishmen by common custom agree upon. And, therefore, to make a change of the English word, as though that all England should go to school with Tindale to learn English, is a very frantic folly.

But now the matter standeth not therein at all; for Tindale is not angry with the word, but because of the matter. For this grieveth Luther and him, that by penance we understand, when we speak thereof so many good things therein, and not a bare repenting or forethinking only, but also every part of the sacrament of penance, confession of mouth, contrition of heart, and satisfaction by good deeds. For, if we called it but the sacrament of repentance, and by that word would understand as much good thereby as we now do by the word penance, Tindale would be then as angry with repentance as he now is with penance. For he hateth nothing but to hear that men should do any good. We have for our poor English word penance the use of all Englishmen since penance first began among them, and that is authority enough for an English word.[1]

FASTING FOR PENANCE AND HUMILIATION.

Tindale and his master (Luther) be wont to cry out upon the Pope and upon all the clergy, for that they meddle[2] philosophy with the things of God, which is a thing that

---

[1] *Conf. of Tindale*, Works, 439.   [2] Mix.

may in place be very well done, since the wisdom of philosophy—all that we find true therein—is the wisdom given of God, and may well do service to His other gifts of higher wisdom than that is. But Tindale here in this place doth lean unto the old natural philosophers altogether; for, as for abstinence to tame the flesh from intemperance, and foul lusts also, this was a thing that many philosophers did both teach and use. But as for fasting, that is another thing, which God hath always among His faithful people had observed and kept, not only for that purpose, but also for a kind of pain, affliction and punishment of the flesh for their sins and to put us in remembrance that we be now in the vale of tears, and not in the hill of joy, saving for the comfort of hope.

And albeit that Tindale be loth to hear thereof, because he would not that any man should do true penance with putting himself to any pain for his own sins, yet would God the contrary. And as He will that men for their sins should be sorry in their hearts, so would He that for the same cause the sorrow of their hearts should redound into their bodies; and that we should, for the provocation of God's mercy, humble ourselves before Him, and not only pray for forgiveness, but also put our bodies to pain and affliction of our own selves, and thereby to show how heavily we take it that we have offended Him.[1]

WORKS OF PENANCE AND SATISFACTION.

Tindale saith God is no tyrant, and thereforth rejoiceth not in our pain but pitieth us, and as it were mourneth with us, and would we should have none, saving that like a good surgeon He putteth pain of tribulation unto the sores of our

---

[1] *Conf. of Tindale*, Works, 368.

sin, because the sin cannot otherwise be rubbed out of the
flesh and cured.

We say not, neither, that God rejoiceth in our pain as a
tyrant, albeit that Luther and Tindale would have us take
Him for such one as had more tyrannous delight in our
pain than ever had tyrant, when they, by the taking away
of man's free will, would make us ween that God alone
worketh all our sin and then damneth His creatures in
perpetual torments for His own deed.

But we say that God rejoiceth and delighteth in the love
of man's heart when He findeth it such as the man inwardly
delighteth in his heart, and outwardly to let the love of his
heart so redound into the body that he gladly by fasting
and other affliction putteth the body to pain for God's sake,
and yet thinketh for all that, that in comparison of his duty
all that is much less than right nought.

We say also that God rejoiceth and delighteth in justice,
and for that cause He delighteth to see a man so delight in
the same, and to take his sin so sorrowfully that he is
content of himself by fasting and other affliction willingly
to put himself to pain therefor.   And I say that if God had
not this delight, which is not a tyrannous but a good and
godly delight, else would He put unto man no pain for sin
at all.   For it is plain false that God doth it for necessity
of driving the sin out of the flesh, as Tindale saith He
doth, because that otherwise it cannot be cured.   For it is
questionless that God can otherwise drive the sin out of the
flesh and by other means cure it, if it so pleased Him, and
so would He, saving for His godly delight in justice, which
He loveth to see man follow by fasting and other penance.[1]

[1] *Conf. of Tindale*, Works, 372.

Heretical Non-Contrition.

Howbeit, Cousin, if so it be, that their [the Lutherans']
way be not wrong, but that they have found out so easy a
way to heaven as to take no thought but make merry ; nor
take no penance at all, but sit them down and drink well
for our Saviour's sake ; sit cock-a-hoop and fill in all the
cups at once, and then let Christ's passion pay for all the
scot—I am not he that will envy their good hap; but surely
counsel dare I give no man to adventure that way with
them. But such as fear lest that way be not sure, and take
upon them willingly tribulation of penance, what comfort
they do take and well may take therein, that have I somewhat told you already. And since these other folk sit so
merry without such tribulation, we need to talk to them,
you wot well, of no such manner of comfort.[1]

Hairshirts.

Then preacheth this " Pacifier " that the clergy should
wear hair. He is surely somewhat sore if he bind them all
thereto ; but among them I think that many do already,
and some whole religion[2] doth. But yet, saith this Pacifier,
that it doth not appear that they do so. Ah ! well said !
But now, if all the lack stand in that point, that such
holiness is hid so that men may not see it, it shall be from
henceforth well done for them, and so they will do if they
be wise, upon this advertisement and preaching of this good
Pacifier, come out of their cloisters every man into the
market place, and there kneel down in the kennel and make

[1] *Dialogue of Comfort*, Works, 1177.
[2] Religious order.

their prayers in the open streets, and wear their shirts of
hair in sight upon their cowls, and then shall it appear, and
men shall see it.   And surely for their shirts of hair in this
way were there none hypocrisy, and yet were there also
good policy, for thus should it not prick them.[1]

THE SEAL OF CONFESSION.

Tindale, in his " Book of Obedience " (or rather of dis-
obedience), saith that the curates[2] do go and show the
bishops the confession of such as be rich in their parishes,
and that the bishops thereupon do cite them and lay their
secret sins to their charge, and either put them to open
shameful penance or compel them to pay at the bishop's
pleasure.   Now dare I be hold to say, and I suppose all
the honest men in this realm will say and swear the same,
that this is a very foolish falsehood, imagined of his own
mind, whereof he never saw the sample in his life. . . .
That priests should utter folks' confession were well possible,
and in many of them nothing in this world more likely
neither, if God and His Holy Spirit were not (as it is)
assistant and working with His Holy Sacrament.   But
surely, whereas there be many things that well and clearly prove
the Sacrament of Confession to be a thing institute and devised by God, yet, if all the remnant lacked, this one thing
were unto me a plain persuasion and a full proof (which
thing I find in the noble book that the king's highness
made against Luther), that is, to wit, that in so common a
custom of confession oftener than once in the year, where
no man letteth boldly to tell such his secrets as, upon the

[1] *Apology*, Works, 896.
[2] Parish priests, all who in any degree had *cure* of souls.

discovering or close keeping thereof, his honesty[1] commonly, and often time his life also, dependeth, so many simple as be of that sort that hear them, and in all other things so light and lavish of their tongue . . . yet find we never any man take harm by his confession, or cause given of complaint, through any such secrets uttered and showed by the confessor.[2]

THE SABBATH-DAY.

Albeit that Christ said unto the Jews that the Son of Man is the Master and Lord over the Sabbath-day, to use it as Himself list, which never listed to use it, but to the best; yet can I not well see Tindale is in such wise master and lord of the Sabbath-day, nor no man else, that he can use it as his man, though it was of God institute for man and not man for it, that is, to wit, for the spiritual benefit and profit of man, as our Saviour saith also Himself. But yet He calleth it not servant unto man, as Tindale calleth it. For the Scripture saith that God hath sanctified the Sabbath-day unto Himself. And that was the cause why that Christ showed unto the Jews that Himself was Lord of the Sabbath-day, because He would that they should thereby know that He was very God, since that they had learned by Scripture that the Sabbath-day was sanctified only to God Himself, for man's profit, and no man lord thereof, but only God. A governor of people is made for the people, and not the people for the governor, and yet is there no man among the people wont to call the governor his man, but himself rather the governor's man. The very Manhood of our Saviour Himself was to

---

[1] Honour. [2] *Dialogue of Comfort*, Works, 294.

some purpose ordained for mankind, as the Incarnation of
His Godhead was ordained for man, but yet useth no wise
man to call Christ his servant, albeit Himself of His meekness did more than serve us.[1]

On Translating the Scripture and Reading it in Vulgar Tongue.

Messenger.—To keep the Scripture from us, the clergy
seek out every rotten reason that they can find, and set
them forth solemnly to the show, though five of those
reasons be not worth a fig. For they begin as far as our
first father Adam, and show us that his wife and he fell out
of paradise with desire of knowledge. Now, if this would
serve, it must from the knowledge and study of Scripture
drive every man, priest and other, lest it drive all out of
paradise.   Then say they that God taught His disciples
many things apart, because the people should not hear it ;
and, therefore, they would the people should not now be
suffered to read all.   Yet they say further, that it is hard to
translate the Scripture out of one tongue into another, and
specially, they say, into ours, which they call a tongue
vulgar and barbarous. But, of all thing, specially they say
that Scripture is the food of the soul, and that the common
people be as infants that must be fed but with milk and
pap; but if we have any stronger meat it must be chammed[2]
afore by the nurse, and so put into the babe's mouth. But methink, though they make us all infants, they shall find many a
shrewd brain among us that can perceive chalk from cheese
well enough ; and if they would once take us our meat in
our own hand, we be not so evil toothed but that within a

---

[1] *Conf. of Tindale*, Works, 373.   [2] Chewed.

while they shall see us cham it ourselves as well as they. For, let them call us young babes and[1] they will, yet by God they shall for all that well find in some of us that an old knave is no child.

More.—Surely such things as ye speak is the thing that (I somewhat said before) putteth good folk in fear to suffer the Scripture in our English tongue; not for the reading and receiving, but for the busy chamming thereof, and for much meddling with such parts thereof as least will agree with their capacities.   For undoubtedly, as ye spake of our mother Eve, inordinate appetite of knowledge is a mean to drive any man out of paradise, and inordinate is the appetite when men unlearned, though they read it in their language, will be busy to ensearch and dispute the great secret mysteries of Scripture, which, though they hear, they be not able to perceive. . . . And thus, in these matters, if the common people might be bold to cham it (as ye say) and to dispute it, then should ye have the more blind the more bold—the more ignorant the more busy—the less wit the more inquisitive—the more fool the more talkative, and this not soberly of any good affection, but presumptuously and unreverently, at meat and at meal.   And there, when the wine were in and the wit out, would they take upon them with foolish words and blasphemy to handle Holy Scripture in more homely fashion than a song of Robin Hood.

Whereas, if we would no further meddle therewith, but well and devoutly read it, and in that that is plain and evident, as God's commandments and His holy counsels, endeavour ourselves to follow, with help of His grace asked

---

[1] If.

thereunto, and in His great and marvellous miracles consider
His Godhead, and in His lowly birth, His godly life, and
His bitter passion exercise ourselves in such meditations,
prayers and virtues as the matter shall minister us occasion,
acknowledging our own ignorance where we find a doubt,
and therein leaning to the faith of the Church, wrestle with
no such text as might bring us in a doubt of any of those
articles wherein every good Christian man is clear ; by this
manner of reading can no man nor woman take hurt in Holy
Scripture.

And to this intent weigh all the words (as far as I perceive) of all holy doctors.   But never meant they (as I
suppose) the forbidding of the Bible to be read in any
vulgar tongue.   Nor I never yet heard any reason laid why
it were not convenient to have the Bible translated into the
English tongue. . . . For as for that our tongue is called
barbarous is but a fantasy ; for so is, as every learned man
knoweth, every strange language to other.   And if they
would call it barren of words, there is no doubt but it is
plenteous enough to express our minds in anything whereof
one man hath used to speak with another.   Now, as touching the difficulty which a translator findeth in expressing
well and lively the sentence of his author, which is hard
always to do so surely but that he shall sometimes minish
either of the sentence [1] or of the grace that it beareth in
the former tongue, that point hath lain in their light that
have translated the Scripture already, either out of Greek
into Latin, or out of Hebrew into any of them both.

Now, as touching the harm that may grow by such blind

---

[1] Meaning.

bayards as will, when they read the Bible in English, be more busy than will become them;—they that touch that point, harp upon the right string and touch truly the great harm that were likely to grow to some folk, howbeit, not by the occasion yet of the English translation, but by the occasion of their own lewdness and folly—which yet were not in my mind a sufficient cause to exclude the translation and to put other folk from the benefit thereof, but rather to make provision against such abuse, and let a good thing go forth. No wise man were there that would put all weapons away because manquellers misuse them. Nor this letted not (as I said) the Scripture to be first written in a vulgar tongue. . . . And of truth seldom hath it been seen that any sect of heretics hath begun of such unlearned folk as nothing could else but the language wherein they read the Scripture; but there hath always commonly these sects sprung of the pride of such folk as had, with the knowledge of the tongue, some high persuasion in themselves of their own learning besides. To whose authority some other folk have soon after, part of malice, part of simpleness, and much part of pleasure and delight in new fangleness fallen in and increased the fashion. But the head hath ever commonly been either some proud, learned man, or, at the least, beside the language, some proud smatterer in learning. Against which things provision must be made that as much good may grow, and as little harm come as can be devised, and not to keep the whole commodity from any whole people because of harm that, by their own folly and fault, may come to some part; as though a lewd[1] surgeon would cut off the

[1] Ignorant.

leg by the knee to keep the toe from the gout, or cut off a
man's head by the shoulders to keep him from the toothache.[1]

FALSE SPIRITUALITY.

"All those things," quoth he, "that were used in the old
law were but gross and carnal, and were all as a shadow of
the law of Christ. And, therefore, the worshipping of God
with gold and silver, and such other corporal things, ought
not to be used among Christian people. For so Christ
saith Himself, that God, as Himself is spiritual, so seeketh
He such worshippers as shall worship Him in spirit and in
truth, that is in faith, hope, and charity of heart, not in the
hypocrisy and ostentation of outward observance, bodily
service, gay and costly ornaments, fair images, goodly song,
fleshly fasting, and all the rabble of such unsavoury
ceremonies, all which are now gone as a shadow."

"These men," quoth I, "that make themselves so
spiritual, God send grace that some evil spirit inspire not to
their hearts a devilish device which, under a cloak of special
zeal to spiritual service, go first about to destroy all such
devotion as ever hath hitherto showed itself, and uttered
the good affection of the soul by good and holy works, unto
God's honour wrought with the body. These men be come
into so high a point of perfection that they pass all the good
men that served God in old time. For as for the good
godly man Moses, he thought that to pray not only in mind,
but with mouth also, was a good way. The good King
David thought it pleasant to God, not only to pray with his

---

[1] *Dialogue of Comfort*, Works, 241-245. More then explains in
detail the precaution that could be taken and the licence given by
bishops to read the Bible, or parts of it, in English.

mouth, but also to sing and dance too, to God's honour; and blamed his foolish wife who did at that time as these foolish heretics do now, mocking that bodily service. St. John the Baptist not only baptised and preached, but also fasted, watched and wore hairshirt. Christ, our Saviour, Himself not only prayed in mind, but also with mouth, which kind of prayer these holy spiritual heretics now call lip-labour in mockery. And the fasting which they set at nought, our Saviour Himself set so much by that He continued it forty days together." [1]

USE OF CHURCHES.

I would well agree that no temple of stone was unto God so pleasant as the temple of man's heart. But yet that nothing letteth or withstandeth but that God will that His Christian people have in sundry places sundry temples and churches, to which they should, beside their private prayers, assemble solemnly and resort in company to worship Him together, such as dwell near together, that they may conveniently resort to one place.

And surely, albeit that some good man here and there, one among ten thousand, as St. Paul and St. Anthony, and a few such other like, do live all heavenly far out of all fleshly company, as far from all occasions of worldly wretchedness as from the common temple or parish church; yet, if churches and congregations of Christ's people resorting together to God's service were once abolished and put away, we were like to have few good temples of God in men's souls, but all would within a while wear away

---

[1] *Dialogue*, Works, 115.

clean and clearly fall to nought. And this prove we by experience, that those which be the best temples of God in their souls they most use to come to the temple of stone. And those that least come there be well known for very ribalds and unthrifts, and openly perceived for the temples of the devil.[1]

CEREMONIES.

Tindale.—And in the ceremonies and sacraments there he captivateth his wit and understanding to obey Holy Church, without asking what they mean or desiring to know, but only careth for the keeping, and looketh ever with a pair of narrow eyes, and with all his spectacles upon them, lest aught be left out.

More.—The ceremonies and sacraments Tindale maketh his mocking-stock. But let him beware betime lest God mock him again. Better is it, good Christian reader, to do the thing that Tindale here reproveth than to do as Tindale hath done, that with his curious search hath so narrowly, so long pryed upon them with beetle brows, and his brittle spectacles of pride and malice, that the devil hath stricken him stark blind, and set him in a corner with a chain and a clog, and made him his ape to sit there and serve him, and to make him sport, with mocking, and mowing, and potting the sacraments, which yet the devil dreadeth himself, and dare not come anear them.[2]

SIGN OF CROSS IN BLESSING.

Tindale.—He had liever that the bishops should wag two fingers over him, than that another man should say: God save him.

---

[1] *Dialogue,* Works, 122.   [2] *Conf. of Tindale,* Works, 398.

More.—Blessing of bishops Tindale jesteth upon in more places than one. And for as much as he knoweth well that all Christian people have, and ever have had, a good faithful belief in blessing, both where a man or woman bless themselves, and also whereas any that hath authority over them, given by God to bless them (which is a kind of prayer and invocation of God's grace upon the party so blessed with the sign of the Cross), as the natural father or the godfather blesseth the child, or the curate his parishioner, or the bishop his diocesan ; such things Tindale taketh for trifles, and laugheth such blessing and crossing to scorn.

St. Gregory Nazianzen writeth that when the great infidel emperor, commonly called Julian the Apostate, was fallen from the faith of Christ unto Paganism, giving himself therewith not only to the persecution of Christian men, but also to the following of every kind of superstitious folly, he took with him on a certain time necromancers and went into a cave to conjure up spirits, to inquire of them certain things whereof he was very curious to know. And when he was in the pit among them with their conjurations, there appeared many terrible sights, so far forth that, albeit with the trust of his conjurations, he bare it out awhile, yet at the last the terror and fear so sore increased, that he was fain for the surest refuge to bless himself with the sign of the Cross, which he so pursued and hated. At which only sign, so made with the wagging (as Tindale calleth it) of the hand in the air, as evil a hand as it was, yet were all the devils so sore afraid, that all their fearful illusions failed and vanished quite away.

And I little doubt that, as little as Tindale setteth by blessing now, yet, if he might once meet the devil in the dark, he would, I warrant you, cross and bless apace. And I beseech our Lord to give him grace to bless himself betimes, that he meet not the devil in eternal darkness, where whoso mishap to meet him can have no grace to cross and bless himself, but shall, instead of crossing, and blessing, fall all to cursing and desperate sorrow and furious blaspheming, without comfort and without end.[1]

Honour Done to Saints.

Surely if any benefit or alms done to one of Christ's poor folk for His sake be ·by His high goodness reputed and accepted as done unto Himself ; and if whoso receiveth one of His apostles or disciples receiveth Himself, every wise man may well consider that in likewise whose doth honour His holy saints for His sake doth honour unto Himself. Except these heretics ween that God were as envious as they be themselves, and that He would be wroth to have any honour done to any other, though it thereby redoundeth unto Himself. Whereof our Saviour Christ well declareth the contrary, for He showeth Himself so well content that His holy saints shall be partners of His honour, that He promiseth His apostles at the dreadful day of doom, when He shall come in His high majesty, they shall have their honourable seats and sit with Himself upon the judgment of the world.

Christ also promised that Saint Mary Magdalen should be worshipped throughout the world, and have here an honourable remembrance for that she bestowed that precious ointment upon His holy head ; which thing, when I consider, it maketh me marvel of the madness of these

[1] *Conf. of Tindale*, Works, 398.

heretics that bark against the old ancient customs of Christ's Church, mocking the setting up of candles, and with foolish facetiousness and blasphemous mockery demand whether God and His saints lack light, or whether it be night with them that they cannot see without candle. They might as well ask what good did that ointment to Christ's head.

But the heretics grudge at the cost now as their brother Judas did then, and say it were better spent in alms upon poor folk ; and this say many of them who can neither find in their heart to spend upon the one or the other ; and some spend sometimes upon the poor for no other intent but that they may the more boldly rebuke and rail against the other. But let them all by that same example of the holy woman, and by these words of our Saviour, learn that God delighteth to see the fervent heat of the heart's devotion boil out by the body and to do Him service with all such goods of fortune as God hath given a man.[1]

CAN SAINTS HEAR US?

Ye marvel and think it hard to be believed that saints hear us. And I (while we see that the things we pray for we obtain) marvel much more how men can doubt whether their prayers be heard or not. When saints were in this world at liberty, and might walk the world about, ween ye that in heaven they stand tied to a post ? " But the wonder is how they may see and hear in sundry places at once." If we, too, could no more but feel, and neither see or hear, we should as well wonder that it were possible for man to see or hear further than he can feel. For we that prove it,

[1] *Dialogue*, Works, 118.

and do see and hear indeed, cannot yet see the cause, nor
in no wise cease to wonder by what reason and mean it may
be, that I should see two churches or two towns, each of
them two a mile asunder, and both twain as far from me as
each of them from other, and measure so great quantities
with so small a measure as is the little apple of mine eye.
And of hearing many men's voices or any man's words,
coming at once into many men's ears standing far asunder,
hath like difficulty to conceive.   And when all the reasons
be made—either of beams sent out from our eyes to the
things that we behold, or the figure of the things seen
multiplied in the air from the thing to our eye, or of the air
stricken with the breath of the speaker, and equally rolling
forth in rondels to the ears of the hearers—when all the
reasons be heard, yet shall we rather delight to search than
be able to find anything in these matters that were able to
make us perceive it.   Now, when we may with our fleshly
eye and ear in this gross body see and hear things far
distant from us, and from sundry places far distant asunder,
marvel we so much that blessed angels and holy souls, being
mere spiritual substances, uncharged of all burdenous flesh
and bones, may in doing the same as far pass and exceed us
and our powers natural, as the lively soul self exceedeth our
deadly body, nor cannot believe that they hear us, though
we find they help us, but if we perceive by what means
they do it, as whether they see and hear us [by] coming
hither to us, or our voice coming hence to them, or
whether God hear and see all and show it them, or whether
they behold it in Him, as one doth in a book the thing that
he readeth, or whether God by some other way doth utter it
unto them as one doth in speaking.   Except we may

know the means we will not else believe the matter. As wise were he that would not believe he can see because he cannot perceive by what means he may see.

"Yet see I (quoth he), no cause or need why we should pray to them, since God can as well and will as gladly both hear us and help us as any saint in heaven." "What need you (quoth I) to pray any physician to help your fever, or pray and pay any surgeon to help your sore leg, since God can hear you and help you both as well as the best, and loveth you better and can do it sooner, and may aforth[1] His plasters better cheap, and give you more for your word than they for your money?" "But this is His pleasure (quoth he) that I shall be holpen by the mean of them as His instruments; though, indeed, all this He doth Himself, since He giveth the nature to the things that they do it with." "So hath it (quoth I) pleased God in likewise that we shall ask help of His holy saints and pray for help to them. Nor, that is not a making of them equal unto God Himself, though they do it by His will and power, or He at their intercession. Though God will (as reason is) be chief and have no match, yet forbiddeth He not one man to pray for help of another. . . . Was Eliseus made equal to God because the widow prayed Him to revive her dead son? And think you, then, that He, being content, and giving men occasion to pray to them while they were on earth, He will be angry if we do them as much worship when they be with Him in heaven? Nay, but I think, on the other side, since His pleasure is to have His saints had in honour and prayed unto . . He will disdain once to look on us if we be so presumptuous and malapert fellows, that upon boldness

[1] Dispense.

of familiarity with Himself we disdain to make our intercessors His especial beloved friends.

"And where St. Paul exhorteth us each to pray for other,
and we be glad to think it well done to pray every poor
man to pray for us, should we think it evil done to pray
holy saints in heaven to the same?" "Why! (quoth he)
by that reason I might pray not only to saints, but also to
every other dead man." "So may ye (quoth I) with good
reason, if ye see none other likelihood but that he died a
good man. And so find we in the Dialogues of St. Gregory,
that one had help by prayer made unto a holy man late
deceased, which was himself yet in purgatory. . . . Those
that be not canonised, ye may for the more part both pray
for them and pray to them, as ye may for and to them
that be yet alive. But one that is canonised ye may pray
to him to pray for you, but ye may not pray for him. . . .
And of every man ye may trust well and be seldom certain,
but of the canonised ye may reckon you sure." [1]

HELP OF ANGELS AND OF SAINTS.

"There appeared unto Him an angel from heaven and
comforted Him" (Luke xxii. 43). Here can I not but
much marvel, what the devil aileth them, that let not to
bear folk in hand that folly were it for a man to desire
either any angel or any saint in heaven to pray unto God
for him, because we may (say they) boldly make our prayer
to God Himself, who alone is more ready to help us than
are the angels and saints, and set them all together. With
such foolish reasons—and, to say truth, nothing to the purpose at all—do these fond fellows, for malice they bear

[2] *Dialogue*, Works, 188-190.

against the honour of saints (and, therefore, may they look for as little favour of them again), go about, as much as they may, both to withdraw our good affection from them, and to take away their wholesome help from us.

Why might not these wretches then with as good reason · say, that the comfort which this angel ministered unto our Saviour Christ, was utterly vain and needless? For, among all the angels in heaven, who was either able to do so much for Him as was Himself alone, or so near at His elbow to assist Him, as was God; and that was He Himself? But like as it pleased His goodness for our sakes to suffer sorrow and anguish; so for our sakes vouchsafed He also by an angel to be comforted, thereby partly to confute these triflers' trifling reasons, and partly to prove Himself to be a very man.[1]

USE OF IMAGES.

The flock of Christ is not so foolish as those heretics hear them in hand, that, whereas there is no dog so mad but he knoweth a very coney[2] from a coney carved and painted, Christian people that have reason in their heads, and thereto the light of faith in their souls, should ween the images of our Lady were our Lady herself. Nay, they be not, I trust, so mad, but they do reverence to the image for the honour of the person whom it representeth, as every man delighteth in the image and remembrance of his friend.

And, albeit that every good Christian man hath a remembering of Christ's passion in his mind, and conceiveth by dumb meditation a form and fashion thereof in his

---

[1] *Treatise on the Passion*, Works, 1368.   [2] Real rabbit.

heart, yet is there no man (I ween) so good nor so well
learned, nor in meditation so well accustomed, but that he
findeth himself more moved to pity and compassion upon
the beholding of the holy crucifix, than when he lacketh it.
And if there be any that, for the maintenance of his opinion,
will peradventure say that he findeth it otherwise in himself, he should give me cause to fear that he hath of Christ's
passion, neither the one way nor the other, but a very faint
feeling ; since that the holy fathers before us did, and all
devout people about us do, find and feel in themselves the
contrary.[1]

PILGRIMAGES.

In the Gospel (John v. 4) where we read that the angel
moved the water, and whoso next went in was cured of his
disease, was it not a sufficient proof that God would they
should come thither for their health ?   Albeit no man can
tell why He sent the angel rather thither, and there did His
miracles than in another water.   But whensoever our Lord
hath in any place wrought a miracle, although He nothing
do it for the place, but for the honour of that saint, whom
He will have honoured in that place, or for the faith that
He findeth with some that prayeth in that place, or for the
increase of faith which He findeth failing and decayed in
that place, needing the show of some miracles for the re-
viving—whatsoever the cause be, yet, I think, the affection
is to be commended of men and women that with good
devotion run thither where they see or hear that our Lord
showeth a demonstration of His special assistance.   And
when He showeth many in one place it is good token that

[1] *Dialogue*, Works, 121.

He would be sought upon, and worshipped there. Many Jews were there that came to Jerusalem to see the miracle that Christ had wrought upon Lazarus, as the Gospel rehearseth. And surely we were worse than Jews, if we would be so negligent, that where God worketh miracle we list not once go move our foot thitherwards. We marvel much that God showeth no more miracles now-a-days, when it is much more marvel that He doth vouchsafe to show any at all among such unkind, slothful, deadly people, as list not once lift up their heads to look thereon, or that our incredulity can suffer Him now-a-days to work any.[1]

Charge of Avarice as Regards Pilgrimages.

"Men reckon," quoth he, "that the clergy is glad to favour these ways, and to nourish this superstition under the name and colour of devotion, to the peril of the people's souls, for the lucre and temporal advantage that themselves receive of the offering."

When I had heard him say what he liked, I demanded if he minded ever to be a priest. Whereunto he answered: "Nay, verily; for methinketh," quoth he, "that there be priests too many already, unless they were better. And, therefore, when God shall send time, I purpose," he said, "to marry." "Well," said I, "then since I am already married twice, and, therefore, can never be a priest, and ye be so set in mind of marriage that ye never will be priest, we two be not the most meekly to ponder what might be said in this matter for the priest's part. Howbeit, when I consider it, methinketh surely that if the thing were such as you say, so far from all frame of right religion and so

[1] *Dialogue*, Works, 123.

perilous to men's souls, I cannot perceive why that the clergy would, for the gain they get thereby, suffer such abusion to continue.

"For first, if it were true that no pilgrimage ought to be used, none image offered unto, nor worship done, nor prayer made unto any saint—then, if none of all these things had ever been in use, or now were all undone, if that were the right way (as I wot well it were wrong) then were it to me little question, but Christian people, being in the true faith, and in the right way to God-ward, would thereby nothing slack their good minds towards the ministers of the Church, but their devotion should toward them more and more increase. So that if they now get by this way one penny they should (if this be wrong and the other right) not fail, instead of a penny now, then to receive a groat.[1]

"Moreover, look me through Christendom, and I suppose ye shall find the fruits of these offerings a right small part of the living of the clergy, and such as—though some few places would be glad to retain—yet the whole body might without any notable loss easily forbear. Let us consider our own country here, and we shall find these pilgrimages for the most part in the hands of such religious persons or such poor parishes as bear no great rule in the Convocations. And besides this, ye shall not find (I suppose) that any bishop in England bath the profit of one groat of any such offering within his diocese. Now standeth then the continuance or the breaking of this manner and custom specially in them who take no profit thereby ; who, if they believed it to be (such as ye call it) superstitious and wicked,

[1] Fourpence.

would never suffer it to continue to the perishing of men's souls, whereby themselves should destroy their own souls, and neither in body nor goods take any commodity.

"And over this we see that the bishops and prelates themselves visit these holy places and pilgrimages with as large offerings and as great cost in coming and going as other people do; so that they not only take no temporal advantage thereof, but also bestow of their own therein.

"And surely I believe this devotion so planted by God's own hand in the hearts of the whole Church, that is, to wit, not the clergy only, but the whole congregation of all Christian people, that if the spiritualty were of the mind to leave it, yet would not the temporalty suffer it.

"Nor if it so were that pilgrimages hanged only upon the covetousness of evil priests—for evil must they be that would for covetousness help the people forward to idolatry—then would not good priests and good bishops have used them theirselves. But I am very sure that many a holy bishop, and therewith excellently well learned in Scripture and the law of God, have had high devotion thereto. . . ." [1]

CALUMNIATING THE CLERGY.

Where this Pacifier saith that "*some say* that all spiritual men as to the multitude do rather induce the people to pilgrimages, pardons, chantries, obits and trentals, than to the payment of their debts, or to restitution of their wrongs, or to the deeds of alms and mercy to their neighbours that are poor and needy, and sometimes too in right extreme necessity"; for my part, I thank God I never yet heard of any one that ever would give that counsel, nor no more, I see well,

[1] *Dialogue of Comfort*, Works, 120.

this Pacifier himself, for he sayeth it but under his common
figure of Some-say. But this would I say, that either he
believed those *some* that so said unto him, or else he
believed them not. If he believed them not, it had been
well done to have left their tale untold till he had believed
them better. And on the other side, if he believed them
well, he might as well with conscience have been less light
of belief, or boldly might have believed that they lied, rather
than lightly believe the lewd words of some, and upon the
malicious mouths of some, blow abroad in books so false a
tale himself against not a small some, but as himself saith as
to the multitude against all spiritual men.[1]

Robbing the Church for the Poor.

Luther wished, in a sermon of his, that he had in his hand
all the pieces of the Holy Cross, and saith that if he so
had, he would throw them there as never sun should shine
on them. And for what worshipful reason would the
wretch do such villany to the Cross of Christ? Because, as
he saith, that there is so much gold now bestowed about
the garnishing of the pieces of the Cross, that there is none
left for poor folk. Is not this a high reason? As though
all the gold that is now bestowed about the pieces of the
Holy Cross would not have failed to have been given to
poor men! And as though there were nothing lost but what
is bestowed about Christ's Cross!

Take all the gold that is spent about all the pieces of
Christ's Cross throughout Christendom—albeit many a good
Christian prince and other goodly people hath honourably
garnished many pieces thereof—yet if all the gold were

[1] *Apology*, ch. xx., Works, 880.

gathered together it would appear a poor portion in comparison of the gold that is bestowed upon cups. What speak we of cups in which the gold, albeit that it be not given to poor men, yet is it saved, and may be given in alms when men will, which they never will? How small a portion were the gold about all the pieces of Christ's Cross if it were compared with the gold that is quite cast away about the gilding of knives, swords, spurs, arras and painted clothes; and, as though these things could not consume gold fast enough, the gilding of posts and whole roses, not only in the palaces of princes and great prelates, but also many right mean men's houses. And yet among all these things could Luther spy no gold that grievously glittered in his bleared eyes, but only about the Cross of Christ. For that gold, if it were taken thence, this wise man weeneth it would be strait given to poor men; and that, when he daily seeth that such as have their purse full of gold give to the poor not one piece thereof. But if they give aught, they ransack the bottom among all the gold to seek out here a halfpenny, or in his country a brass penny, whereof four make a farthing. Such goodly causes find they that pretend holiness for the colour of their cloaked heresies.[1]

A Calumny.

Now when Tindale asketh me why the bishop selleth the oil unto the curates wherewith they anoint the sick; thereto I say that the bishop sendeth it to the curates because they should therewith anoint the sick in the sacrament of anoiling. But why he *selleth* it to the curates, if he so did, thereof can I not tell the cause, but if it were peradventure

[1] *Dialogue*, Works, 119.

because he would be paid therefor. But I can tell well that
the bishop selleth it *not* to curates, nor no man else, but the
curates have it sent them free ; but if they reward the
bringer of their courtesy with a groat, which bringer is yet
the archdeacon's servant and not the bishop's. And this I
can tell, for I have inquired for the nonce, and by this can
I tell as well that Tindale here belieth the bishop shamefully for the nonce.[1]

The Fire of Hell.

Verely it seemeth that they would set the people upon
mirth ; for penance they shake off as a thing not necessary,
satisfaction they call great sin, and confession they call the
devil's drift. And of purgatory by two means they put men
out of dread ; some by sleeping till doomsday, and some by
sending all straight to heaven, every soul that dieth and is not
damned for ever. And yet some good comfort give they to
the damned too. For till they see some time to deny hell
all utterly, they go about in the mean season to put out the
fire. And some yet boldly forthwith to say there is none
there, *that* they dread a little, and therefore for the season
they bring the matter in question and dispute it abroad, and
say they will not utterly affirm and say the contrary, but
the thing is, they say, but as *problema neutrum*, wherein
they would not force [*care*] whether part they should take ;
and if they should choose they would rather hold nay than
yea ; or, though there be fire in either place, that yet it
neither burneth soul in hell nor paineth soul in purgatory.

But Christ (I wot well) in many places saith there is fire
there, and His holy saints after Him affirm and say the

[1] *Conf. of Tindale*, Works, 431.

same, and with the fire He fraid [*caused to fear*] His own disciples, bidding them fear that fire that they fall not therein.

For, though that clerks may in schools hold problems
upon everything, yet can I not perceive what profit there
can come to call it but a problem among unlearned folk,
and dispute it out abroad, and bring the people in doubt,
and make them rather think that there is none than any,
and that this word fire is spoken but by parable, as those
men make the eating of Christ's blessed body. Thus shall
they make men take both paradise and heaven, and God
and all together but for parables at last.

Though fear of hell alone be but a servile dread, yet are
there already too many that fear hell too little, even of them
that believe the truth, and think that in hell there is very
fire indeed. How many will there be that will fear it less if
such words once may make them ween that there were in
hell no very fire at all, but that the pain that they shall feel
in hell were but after the manner of some heavy mind or of
a troublous dream ?

If a man believe Christ's word that in hell is fire indeed,
and make the fear of that fire one means to keep him
thence, then, though there were no fire there, yet hath he
nothing lost, since good he can get none there though the
fire were thence. But if he believe such words on the other
side, and catch thereby such boldness that he set hell at
light, and by the means thereof fall boldly to sin, and thereupon finally fall down unto the devil; if he then find fire there,
as I am sure he shall, then shall he lie there and curse
them that told him those false tales, as long as God with
His good folk sitteth in the heaven.[1]

[1] *Answer to the Masker*, Works, 1120.

THE MAINTAINERS AND DENYERS OF PURGATORY.

Surely, if three or four hundred good and honest men would faithfully come forth and tell one that some of his friends were in a far country for debt kept in prison, and that his charity might relieve them thence ; if then, three or four fond fellows would come and say the contrary, and tell him plain there is no such prison at all ; if he would now be so light as to believe those three or four naughty persons against those three or four hundred good and honest men, he then should well decipher himself, and well declare thereby that he would gladly catch hold of some small handle to keep his money fast, rather than help his friends in their necessity.

Now, if these men will peradventure say that they care not for such comparison neither of time with time, number with number, nor company with company, but—since some one man is in credence with some seven score--if they will, therefore, call us to some other reckoning and will that we compare of the best choice on both sides a certain,[1] and match them man for man ; then have we (if we might for shame match such blessed saints with a sort so far unlike) St. Austin against Friar Luther, St. Jerome against Friar Lambert, St. Ambrose against Friar Huskin [Œcolampadius], St. Gregory against Friar Pomerane, St. Chrysostom against Tindale, and St. Basil against the Beggars' proctor (Simon Fish).

Now, if our enemies will, for lack of other choice, help forth their own part with their wives, then have they some advantage indeed, for the other holy saints had none.   But

---

[1] A certain is a selection, a certain number.

yet shall we not lack blessed holy women against these friars' wives. For we shall have St. Anastasia against Friar' Luther's wife, St. Hildegard against Friar Huskin's wife, St. Bridget against Friar Lambert's wife, and St. Catharine of Siena against Priest Pomerane's wife.[1]

PURGATORY AND INDULGENCES.

Tindale.—"What great fear can there be of that terrible fire, which thou mayst quench almost for three halfpence?"

More.—Nay, surely, that fire is not so lightly quenched that folk should upon the boldness of pardons stand out of the fear of purgatory. For likewise, as though the sacrament of penance be able to put away the eternality of the pain, yet hath the party for all that cause to fear both purgatory and hell too, lest some default upon his own part letted God in the sacrament to work such grace in him as should serve therefor; so, though the pardon be able to discharge a man of purgatory, yet may there be such default in the party to whom the pardon is granted, though he give for [instead of] three halfpence, three hundred pounds, yet shall he receive no pardon at all. And, therefore, can he not be for three halfpence out of fear of purgatory, but ever hath cause to fear it. For no man, except revelation, can be sure whether he be partner of the pardon or not, though he may have, and ought to have, both in that and every good thing, good hope.

And if the fear of purgatory were so clear gone, because it might be quenched with the cost of three halfpence, then were the fear of hell gone, too, by Tindale's teaching, since

[1] *Supplication of Souls*, Works, 330.

bare faith and slight repentance putteth out that fire clean without the cost of a penny.[1]

PRIVILEGES OF MARTYRDOM.

If I should hap to find a man that had long lived a very virtuous life, and had at last happed to fall into the Turks' hands, and there did abide by the truth of his faith and with the suffering of all kind of torments taken upon his body, still did teach and testify the truth; if I should in his passion give him spiritual comfort, might I be bold to tell him no farther, but that he should take patience in his pain, and that God sendeth it him for his sin, and that he is well worthy to have it, although it were yet much more? He might then well answer me, and such other comforters, as Job answered his: " Burdenous and heavy comforters be you ". Nay, I would not fail to bid him boldly, while I should see him in his passion, cast sin, and hell, and purgatory, and all upon the devil's pate, and doubt not, but like as if he gave over his hold all his merit were lost, and he turned to misery; so if he stand and persevere still in the confession of his faith all his whole pain shall turn all into glory.

Yea, more shall I yet say than this : that if there were a Christian man that had among those infidels committed a very deadly crime, such as were worthy death not by their laws only but by Christ's too, as manslaughter or adultery, or such other thing like, if when he were taken he were offered pardon of his life upon condition that he should forsake the faith of Christ; if this man would now rather suffer death than so do, should I comfort him in his pain

[1] *Conf. of Tindale*, Works, 476.

but as I would a malefactor? Nay, this man, though he should have died for his sin, dieth now for Christ's sake while he might live still if he would forsake Him. The bare patient taking of his death should have served for satisfaction of his sin, through the merit of Christ's passion, I mean, without help of which no pain of our own could be satisfactory. But now shall Christ for his forsaking of his own life in the honour of His faith forgive the pain of all his sins of His mere liberality, and accept all the pain of his death for merit of reward in heaven, and shall assign no part thereof to the payment of his debt in purgatory, but shall take it all as an offering, and requite it all with glory; and this man among Christian men, all had he been before a devil, nothing after would I doubt to take him for a martyr.[1]

FREE WILL.

Every good Christian man seeth well enough that the Lutherans are wickedly occupied in seeking (as David says) excuses for their sin. For there is no man that doth such deeds against his will. And therefore, when Tindale telleth us that Luther and he, and such other true members of their Church, "when they commit such horrible deeds, do not commit them willingly," because they commit them "on great occasions," and be carried away spite of their teeth "with the rage of the sin that breaketh out of their members"; saving my charity, sir, I bestrew their knavish members. Let them cast on cold water with sorrow and quench the rage.[2]

[1] *Dialogue of Comfort*, Works, 1150.
[2] *Conf. of Tindale*, Works, 555.

PREDESTINATION TO EVIL.

If his [Barns'] own secret hostess, the good wife of the
Bottle, of Botolph's Wharf, that (but if she be better
amended) halteth both in body and soul, were in the
congregation, and then would hymp[1] forth among them and
say: " By St. Malkin,[2] Father Barns, all your tokens of the
very true Church will not stand me in the stead of a tavern
token,[3] nor of a mustard token neither.   For I may for the
one be sure of a new-baken bun, and for the other I may
be sure of a pot of mustard ; but for your two tokens of
your holy Church I cannot be sure of one farthing-worth of
true doctrine for them both.   For how shall I perceive that
any true members of your holy Church (in only whom ye
say is the true faith) be present in company when your
tokens be (*a*) the true preaching of Scripture, and (*b*) the
good living after the Scripture ?   How can I get any good
by those two tokens when I cannot read at all ? "

What could Friar Barns say to his hostess here ?   Surely
nothing hath he, but should in the end be fain to fall to the
destiny of God's election, and say that when they come to
the preaching all those that are elect of God shall be
secretly moved and taught inwardly, and shall, by the
instinct of the Spirit of God, though they know not whether
the person be good or no that preacheth, perceive yet the
true word of God upon the hearing, and shall understand it,
as Tindale saith that the eagle perceiveth her prey.   And
the other sort, whom God doth not choose, though they
hear it shall not understand it, but, whether the preacher
be good or bad, they shall be never the better, nor shall not

---

[1] *i.e.*, limp   [2] A fantastic oath.   [3] Sign—signboard.

discern the true preacher from the false, but be deceived by the false, and not perceive the true, for anything that they can do. And here this anchor in conclusion shall he be fain to cast out, with which, when he would ween to stay the ship, he draweth it quite under the water. For I ween his hostess would soon have said somewhat thereto. For I wot well she is not tongue-tied; I have heard her talk myself.

She would, I ween, therefore have said unto him thus much at the leastwise · "Why, Father Barns, when God calleth upon us all, and we come together at His calling, and my neighbour and I come both to Church with one purpose—to learn the right way to heaven—would you make me ween that God were so partial that, without any difference of cause between her and me, I being as well willing to learn to please Him as she, that when I have at His calling followed Him so far as well as she (and with somewhat more pain, too, for I halt, ye wot well), He will, for all that I halt, make her perceive the truth, and go forth farther with Him, till He bring her to heaven, and leave me still in darkness and ignorance, and let me fall into hell, for none other cause but only for He list to choose her and leave me unchosen? If He gave her more than me for His only pleasure, I could find no fault. But, marry, sir, that He would give her all, and me not only nothing, but also condemn me to perpetual fire, because Himself would not cause me to perceive the truth; and no cause why He would not, but because He would not choose me, and no cause why He would not choose me, but only because He would not :—in good faith, I take God for so good that I can never believe you therein. . . . It were an evil master that

would call many children to school, and when he had them
there, then set divers ushers under him to teach them, and
would make some, whom he favoured causeless, to be taught
right, and suffer some, whom he hated as causeless, to be taught
wrong, and after come and hear all their lessons himself, and
those that have been taught right, make much of them and
cherish them because they say right, and those that have been
wrong taught, all to chide them and beat them because they
say wrong. In good faith, Father Barns, I take God for so
good, that I cannot believe that He would do so. But
rather, as these common preachers[1] say, that God hath provided sufficient learning for all sorts, of which they may be
sure if they will come to it," etc.[2]

PRACTICAL ADVICE IN CONTROVERSIES.

Now, if any man will bear other in hand that this point
or that point is not determined,[3] or that the doctors of the
Church write not in such wise, but the contrary, then, whosoever is not of such learning as to perceive by himself
whether of these two say true that hold therein contrary
parts, then, except the article be a plain, open, known thing
of itself, not doubted of before, let him not be light of
evidence in the believing either the one disputer or the
other, though they would both preach high praises of their
own cunning, and say that, beside all their much worldly
business, they had spent many years about the study of
Scripture, and boast that their books of divinity were worth
never so much money, or that by the spirit they were in-

[1] Catholic priests.

[2] *Conf. of Tindale*, book viii., Works, 766.

[3] The context shows that the meaning is that there has been no
definition or clear teaching of the Church on the subject.

spired, and with the celestial dew suddenly sprung up divines, as lusty, fresh, and green as after any shower of rain ever sprung any bed of leeks. Let no man (I say) be light in believing them for all that, but let him, by my poor counsel, pray God inspire himself to believe and follow the thing that may be His high pleasure, and let him thereupon appoint with himself to live well, and forthwith to begin well, get himself a good ghostly father, and shrive him of his sins; and then, concerning the question, ask advice and counsel of those whom himself thinketh, between God and his new cleansed conscience, for learning and virtue most likely, without any partial leaning, indifferently to tell him the truth.[1]

LAST WORDS OF BLESSED MORE'S CONTROVERSIAL WORKS.

Of whose false, wily folly to beware our Lord give us grace, and of all such other like, which with foolish arguments of their own blind reason, wresting the Scripture into a wrong sense against the very plain words of the text, against the exposition of all the old holy saints, against the determination of divers whole general councils, against the full consent of all true Christian nations this fifteen hundred years before their days, and against the plain declaration of Almighty God Himself made in every Christian country by so many plain, open miracles, labour now to make us so foolishly blind and mad as to forsake the very true Catholic faith, forsake the society of the true Catholic Church, and with sundry sects of heretics fallen out thereof to set both holy days and fasting days at naught, and for the devil's pleasure to forbear and abstain from all prayer to be made either for souls or to saints, jest on our Blessed Lady,

[1] *Apology*, Works, 927.

the immaculate Mother of Christ, make mocks of all
pilgrimages and creeping to Christ's Cross, the holy ceremonies of the Church and the sacraments too, turn them
into trifling with likening them to wine garlands and ale
poles ; and, finally, by these ways, in the end and conclusion, forsake our Saviour in the blessed sacrament, and
instead of His own blessed body and blood, ween there
were nothing but bare bread and wine, and call it idolatry
there to do Him honour.

But woe may such wretches be l For this we may be
sure, that whoso dishonour God in one place with occasion
of a false faith,—standing that false belief and infidelity,
all honour that he doeth Him anywhere beside is odious
and despiteful and rejected of God, and never shall save
that faithless soul from the fire of hell.   From which, our
Lord, give them grace truly to turn in time, so that we and
they together in one Catholic Church knit unto God together in one Catholic faith—faith, I say, not faith alone as
they do, but accompanied with good hope and with her
chief sister well-working charity, may so receive Christ's
blessed sacraments here, and specially that we may so
receive Himself, His very blessed body, very flesh and
blood, in the blessed sacrament, our holy blessed housel,
that we may here be with Him incorporate so by grace, that
after the short course of this transitory life, with His tender
pity poured upon us in purgatory, at the prayer of good
people and intercession of holy saints, we may be with them
in their holy fellowship incorporate in Christ in His eternal
glory.   Amen.

End of Fifth Book of *Treatise on Blessed Sacrament against the Masker,*
Works, 1138.

PART THE THIRD.

ILLUSTRATIVE OF THE PERIOD.

LONDON WONDERS.

More.—Who would not ween it impossible, but if experience had proved it, that the whole earth hangeth in the air, and men walk foot against foot, and ships sail bottom against bottom, a thing so strange, and seeming so far against nature and reason that Lactantius, a man right wise and well learned, in his work which he writeth—*De divinis institutionibus*—reckoneth it for impossible, and letteth not to laugh at the philosophers for affirming of the point ; which is yet now founden true by experience of them that have in less than two years sailed the world round about ?

It is not yet fifty years ago since the first man, as far as men have heard, came to London, that ever parted the gilt from the silver, consuming shortly the silver into dust with a very fair water. In so far forth, that when the finers and goldsmiths of London heard first thereof they nothing wondered thereof but laughed thereat as at an impossible lie, in which persuasions, if they had continued still, they had yet at this day lacked all that cunning.

Yet will I not say nay but that a man may be light in belief and be by such ensamples brought in to believe too far. As a good fellow and friend of mine late, in talking of this matter of marvels and miracles, intending merrily to make me believe for a truth a thing that could never be, first brought in what a force the fire hath that will make two pieces of iron able to be joined and cleave together, and with the help of the hammer be made both one, which no hammering could do without the fire. Which thing, because I daily see, I assented. Then, said he, further, that it was more marvel that the fire should make iron to run as silver or lead doth, and make it take a print. Which thing I told him I had never seen, but because he had seen it I thought it to be true. Soon after this, he would have me to believe that he had seen a piece of silver of two or three inches about, and in length less than a foot, drawn by man's hand through strait holes made in an iron till it was brought in thickness not half-an-inch about, and in length drawn out I cannot tell how many yards. And when I heard him say that he saw this himself, then I wot well he was merrily disposed.

Messenger.—Marry, it was high time to give him over when he came to that.

More.—Well, what if I should tell you now that I had seen the same?

Messenger.—By my faith, I would believe it at leisure when I had seen the same, and in the meanwhile I could not let you to say your pleasure in your own house; but I would think you were disposed merrily to make me a fool.

More.—Well, what if there would, besides me, ten or twenty good honest men tell you the same tale, and that they had all seen the thing done themselves?

Messenger.—In faith, since I am sent hither to believe you, I would in that point believe yourself alone, as well as them all.

More.—Well, ye mean ye would believe us all alike.

But what would you then say if one or twain of them would say more?

Messenger.—Marry, then would I believe the less.

More.—What if they would show you that they have seen that the piece of silver was over-gilt, and the same piece being still drawn through the holes, the gilt not rubbed off, but still go forth in length with the silver, so that all the length of many yards was gilded of the gilding of the first piece not a foot long?

Messenger.—Surely, sir, those twain that would tell me so much more I would say were not so cunning in the maintenance of a lie as was the pilgrim's companion, which, when his fellow had told at York that he had seen of late at London a bird that covered all Paul's churchyard with his wings, coming to the same place on the morrow, said that he saw not that bird, but he heard much speech thereof: but he saw in Paul's churchyard an egg so great that ten men could scant move it with levers. This fellow could help it forth with a proper side way. But he were no proper underpropper of a lie that would minish his credence with affirming all the first, and setting a louder lie thereto.

More.—Well, then I have espied if ten should tell you so, you would not believe them.

Messenger.—No, not if twenty should.

More.—What if a hundred would that seem good and credible?

Messenger.—If they were ten thousand they were not of credence with me when they should tell me that they saw the thing that myself knoweth by nature and reason impossible. For, when I know it could not be done, I know well that they lie all, be they never so many, that say they saw it done.

More.—Well, since I see well ye would not in this point believe a whole town, ye have put me to silence, that I dare not now be bold to tell you that I have seen it myself. But surely, if witness would have served me, I ween I might have brought you a great many good men that would say and swear too that they have seen it themselves. But now shall I provide me to-morrow peradventure a couple of witnesses of whom I wot well ye will mistrust neither.

Messenger.—Who be they? for it were hard to find whom I could better trust than yourself, whom, whatsoever I have merrily said, I could not in good faith but believe you in that you should tell me earnestly upon your own knowledge. But ye use (my master saith) to look so sadly [seriously] when ye mean merrily, that many times men doubt whether ye speak in sport when ye mean good earnest.

More.—In good faith I mean good earnest now; and yet as well as ye dare trust me, I shall as I said, if ye will go with me, provide a couple of witnesses of whom ye will believe any one better than twain of me, for they be your own friends, and ye have been better acquainted with them, and such as, I dare say for them, be not often wont to lie.

Messenger.—Who be they, I pray you?

More.—Marry, your own two eyes; for I shall, if you will, bring you where you shall see it, no further hence than even here in London. And as for iron and laten [brass] to be so drawn in length, ye shall see it done in twenty shops almost in one street.[1]

STRANGENESS.

More.—We wonder nothing at the ebbing and flowing of

[1] *Dialogue*, Works, 126.

the sea or the Thames because we daily see it. But he that had never seen it nor heard thereof would at the first sight wonder sore thereat, to see that great water come wallowing up against the wind, keeping a common course to and fro, no cause perceived that driveth it. If a man born blind had suddenly his sight, what wonder would he make to see the sun, the moon and the stars ; whereas one that hath seen them sixteen years together, marvelleth not so much of them all, as he would wonder at the very first sight of a peacock's tail.

If ye never had seen any gun in your days nor heard of any before, if two men should tell you, the one that he had wist [known] a man in a Pater Noster while[1] conveyed and carried a mile off, from one place to another by miracle, and the other should tell you that he had seen a stone more than a man's weight carried more than a mile in as little space by craft, which of these would you, by your faith, take for the more incredible? Surely, quoth he, both twain were very strange. But yet I could not choose but think it were rather true that God did the one than that any craft of man could do the other.[2]

True and False Miracles.

Messenger.—Some priest, to bring up a pilgrimage in his parish, may devise some false fellow feigning himself to come seek a saint in his church, and there suddenly say that he hath gotten his sight. Then shall ye have the bells rung for a miracle, and the fond folk of the country soon made fools. Then women coming thither with their

---

[1] During the space of time required to say the " Our Father ".

[2] *Dialogue*, Works, 132.

candles, and the parson, buying of some lame beggars three
or four pair of their old crutches, with twelve pence spent in
men and women of wax, thrust through divers places, some
with arrows and some with rusty knives, will make his
offerings for one seven year worth twice his tithes.

More.—There is very truth that such things may be, and
sometimes so be indeed.   I have heard my father tell of a
beggar[1] that in King Henry's days, the sixth, came with his
wife to St. Alban's, and there was walking about the town
begging, a five or six days before the king's coming thither,
saying that he was born blind and never saw in his life, and
was warned in his dream that he should come out of
Berwick, where he said he had ever dwelled, to seek St.
Alban, and there he had been at his shrine and had not
been holpen.   And therefore he would go seek him at some
other place, for he had heard some say, since he came, that
St. Alban's holy body should be at Cologne, and, indeed,
such a contention hath there been.   But of truth, as I am
surely informed, he lieth here at St. Alban's, saving some
relics of him which they there show shrined.

But to tell you forth.   When the king was come, and the
town full, suddenly this blind man at St. Alban's shrine had
his sight again, and a miracle solemnly rung and "Te Deum"
sung, so that nothing was talked of in all the town but this
miracle.   So happened it then, that Duke Humphrey, of
Gloucester, a great wise man and very well learned, having
great joy to see such a miracle, called the poor man unto
him.   And, first showing himself joyous of God's glory, so
showed in the getting of his sight, and exhorting him to

---

[1] This story has been introduced by Shakespeare into the Second
Part of *Henry VI.*, act ii. scene 1.

meekness and to non-ascribing of any part [of] the worship[1]
to himself, nor to be proud of the people's praise, which
would call him a good and goldly man thereby. At last
he looked well upon his eyes, and asked whether he could
never see nothing at all in all his life before. And when as
well his wife as himself affirmed fastly no, then he looked
advisedly upon his eyes again and said : " I believe you
very well, for methinketh that ye cannot see well yet ".
"Yes, sir" (quoth he), "I thank God and his holy martyr I
can see now as well as any man." " Ye can ? " quoth the
duke ; " what colour is my gown ? " When anon the
beggar told him, " What colour," quoth he, " is this man's
gown ? " He told him also, and so forth without any
sticking he told him the names of all the colours that could
be showed him. And when my lord saw that, he bade him
walk faitor,[2] and made him be set openly in the stocks.
For though he could have seen suddenly by miracle the
difference between divers colours, yet could he not by the
sight so suddenly tell the names of all these colours, but if
he had known them before, no more than the names of all
the men that he should suddenly see.[3]

After this and other tales of imposture, Sir Thomas shows that
false miracles neither disprove true miracles, nor make all miracles
doubtful, but merely show the necessity of precaution and of proper
tests.

I am sure, though ye see some white sapphire or berill
so well counterfeit, and so set in a ring, that a right good
jeweller will take it for a diamond, yet will ye not doubt for
all that, but that there be in many other rings already set

---

[1] *i.e.*, honour or merit.   [2] *i.e.*, stand forth as an impostor.
[3] *Dialogue*, Works, 134.

right diamonds indeed. Nor ye will not mistrust St. Peter for Judas. Ye be wiser than the gentlewoman was, which, in talking once with my father, when she heard say that our Lady was a Jew, first could not believe it, but said : "What ! ye mock, I wis. I pray you tell truth !" And when it was so fully affirmed that she at last believed it, "And was she a Jew ?" quoth she ; "so help me God and halidom, I shall love her the worse while I live". I am sure ye will not so, nor mistrust all for some, neither men nor miracles. Among miracles I durst boldly tell you for one the wonderful work of God that was within these few years wrought in the house of a right worshipful knight, Sir Roger Wenworth, upon divers of his children, and specially one of his daughters, a very fair young gentlewoman of twelve years of age, in marvellous manner vexed and tormented by our ghostly enemy the devil, her mind alienated and raving with despising and blasphemy of God, and hatred of all hallowed things, with knowledge and perceiving of the hallowed from the unhallowed, all were she nothing warned thereof. And after that, moved in her own mind, and monished by the will of God, to go to our Lady of Ipswich. In the way of which pilgrimage she prophesied and told many things done and said at the same time in other places, which were proved true ; and many things said lying in her trance, of such wisdom and learning that right cunning men highly marvelled to hear of so young an unlearned maiden, when herself wist not what she said, such things uttered and spoken as well-learned men might have missed with a long study. And finally, being brought and laid before the image of our Blessed Lady, was there, in the sight of many worshipful people, so grievously tormented, and in face, eyes, look, and countenance so grisly changed, with her mouth drawn aside and her eyes laid out upon her cheeks, that it was a terrible sight to behold. And after many marvellous things at that same time showed upon divers persons by the devil, through God's sufferance, as well all the remnant as the maiden herself, in the presence of all the company restored to their good state perfectly cured and suddenly.

And in this matter no pretext of begging; no suspicion of feigning, no possibility of counterfeiting; no simpleness in the seers; her father and mother right honourable and rich, sore abashed to see such chances in their children; the witnesses great number, and many of great worship, wisdom and good experience; the maid herself too young to feign, and the fashion itself too strange for any man to feign. And the end of the matter virtuous, the virgin so moved in her mind with the miracle that she forthwith, for aught her father could do, forsook the world and professed religion in a very good and godly company of the Minoresses, where she hath lived well and graciously ever since.[1]

Superstitious Devotion to Saints.

Messenger. — Some saints serve for the eye only and some for a sore breast; St. Germain only for children, and yet will he not even look at them, but if the mother bring with them a white loaf and a pot of good ale. And yet is he wiser than St. Wilgefort, for the good soul is (as they say) served and content with oats; whereof I cannot perceive the reason, but if it be because she would

[1] *Dialogue*, Works, 137.

provide a horse for an evil husband to ride to the devil upon. For that is the thing that she is to be sought for, as they say. Insomuch that women hath therefore changed her name, and instead of Wilgefort call her St. Uncumber, because they reckon that for a peck of oats she will not fail to uncumber them of their husbands.

More.—In good faith somewhat indeed it is you say; for evil it is and evil it is suffered, that superstitious manner of worship. Touching the offering of bread and ale to St. Germain, I see nothing much amiss therein. I have myself seen sometimes, yet am I not remembered that ever I saw priest or clerk fare the better therefor, or once drink thereof; but is given to children or poor folk to pray for the sick child. And I would ween it were none offence in such fashion to offer up a whole ox and distribute it among poor people.

We will come to Paul's[1] and the superstitious manner and unlawful petitions. If women there offer oats unto St. Wilgefort, in trust that they shall uncumber them of their husbands, yet can neither the priests perceive, till they find it there, that the foolish women bring oats thither; nor is it not, I think, so often done, nor so much brought at once, that the church may make much money of it above the finding of[2] the canons' horses.

Messenger.—Nay all the oats of a whole year's offering will not find three geese and a gander a week together.

More.—Well then the priests maintain not the matter for any great covetise, and also that the peevish women pray they cannot hear. Howbeit if they pray but to be uncumbered meseemeth no great harm nor unlawfulness therein.

[1] St. Paul's Cathedral, London.   [2] Providing for.

For that may they by more ways than one. They may be uncumbered if their husbands change their cumbrous conditions or if they themselves peradventure change their cumbrous tongues, which is haply the cause of all their cumbrance; and finally, if they cannot be uncumbered but by death, yet it may be by their own, and so their husbands safe enough.

Messenger.—Nay, nay, ye find them not such fools, I warrant you. They make their covenants in their bitter prayers as surely as [if] they were penned, and will not cast away their oats for nought.

More.—Well, to all these matters is one evident easy answer, that they nothing touch the effect of our matter, which standeth in this, whether the thing that we speak of, as praying to saints, going to pilgrimage and worshipping relics and images, may be done well, not whether it may be done evil. . . . And touching the evil petitions, though they that ask them were (as I trust they be not) a great people,[1] they be not yet so many that ask evil petitions of saints, as there be that ask the same of God Himself; for whatsoever they will ask of any good saint they will ask of God also. . . . Shall we therefore find a fault with every man's prayer, because thieves pray for speed in robberies?[2]

An Image with Relics.

Myself saw at the Abbey of Barking, beside London, to my remembrance about thirty years past,[3] in the setting an old image in a new tabernacle, the back of the image being all plated over, and of long time before laid with beaten gold,

[1] Multitude.   [2] *Dialogue*, Works, 194-199.
[3] Sir Thomas writes in 1528.

happened to erase[1] in one place, and out there fell a pretty little door, at which fell out also many relics that had been unknown in that image God wot how long ; and as long had been likely to lie again if God by that chance had not brought them to light.   The Bishop of London[2] came then thither to see there were no deceit therein.   And I among others was present there while he looked thereon and examined the matter.   And in good faith it was to me a marvel to behold the manner of it.   I have forgotten much thereof, but I remember a little piece of wood there was rudely shaped in cross, with thread wrapped about it. Writing had it none, and what it was we could not tell, but it seemed as new cut as if it had been done within one day before.   And divers relics had old writings on them and some had none, but among others were there certain small kerchiefs which were named there our Lady's, and of her own working.   Coarse were they not, nor they were not large, but served as it seemed to cast in a plain and simple manner upon her head.   But surely they were as clean seams to my seeming as ever I saw in my life, and were therewith as white for all that long lying as if they had been washed and laid up within one hour.   And how long that image had standen in that old tabernacle that could no man tell, but there had in all the church none as they thought standen longer untouched.   And they guessed that four or five hundred years ago the image was hidden when the abbey was burned by infidels, and those relics hidden therein, and after the image found and set up many years after when they were gone that had hid it.[3]

---

[1] Crack.   [2] The Bishop in 1498 was Thomas Savage.
[3] *Dialogue*, Works, 192.

FORMER HATRED OF HERESY.

This decay from chastity by declination into foul and filthy talking hath begun a great while ago, and is very far grown on. But the time hath been even until now very late that, albeit of fleshly wantonness, men have not letted to use themselves in words both lewd and very large ; yet of one thing ever would every good man be well ware, that heresy would he no man suffer to talk at his table, but would both rebuke and detect it too, although the thing touched his own born brother. Such hath been till of late the common Christian zeal towards the Catholic faith.[1]

ATHEISTS.

The prophet testifieth : "The fool hath said in his heart there is no God". With the mouth the most foolish will forbear to say it unto other folk, but in the heart they let not to say it softly to themselves. And I fear me there be many more such fools than every man would ween there were, and would not let to say it openly too, if they forbore it not more for the dread of shame of men, than for any fear of God.[2]

THE CARTHUSIANS.

As for the monks of the Charterhouse, would God we were no farther from very virtuous devotion than these good men be from unlawful superstition, among whom, God be thanked, we see many live to very great age, and never heard I yet any died for lack of eating flesh, and yet heard I never that any of them have eaten any, saving some such

[1] *Answer to the Masker*, Works, 1035.
[2] *Dialogue of Comfort*, Works, 1230.

as have come from their cloisters into Luther's Church, as
Otho did in Almain, which ran out of the Charterhouse,
and left fish, and fell to flesh altogether, and took a wife
for soberness and chastising of his monkly members, as
Tindale speaketh.[1]

CONFISCATION OF CHURCH PROPERTY.

To say the truth, much marvel have I to see some folk
now so much and so boldly speak of taking away any possessions of the clergy. For, albeit that once in the time of
the famous prince, King Henry IV., about the time of a
great rumble that the heretics made, when they would have
destroyed, not the clergy only, but the king also and his
nobility too, there was a foolish bill and a false put into a
parliament or twain, and sped as they were worthy ; yet had
I never founden in all my time while I was conversant in
the court, of all the nobility of this land above the number
of seven (of which seven there are now three dead) that
ever I perceived to be of the mind, that it were either right
or reasonable, or could be to the realm profitable, without
lawful cause, to take any possessions away from the clergy,
which good and holy princes and other devout virtuous
people, of whom there be now many blessed saints in
heaven, have, of devotion toward God, given to the clergy,
to serve God and pray for all Christian souls.[2]

We be sure enough that good men were they that gave

---

[1] *Conf. of Tindale*, Works, 397.

[2] *Apology*, Works, 885. More elsewhere notes that he speaks
disjunctively. He does not assert that he knew seven or even one
who maintained that it was right to confiscate Church property. If
seven had said it would be profitable, provided it were lawful, his
words would be true.

this gear into the Church, and therefore naught[1] should they be of likelihood, that would pull it out thence again. To which ravin and sacrilege our Lord (we trust) shall never suffer this realm to fall. Holy St. Austin, in his days, when he perceived that some evil people murmured at the possessions that then were given into his church, did, in an open sermon among all the people, offer them their lands again, and that his church and he would forsake them, and bade them take them who would. And yet there was not found in all that town—albeit that these people were (as these Africans be) very barbarous, fierce, and boisterous[2]—yet was there none, as we say, found any one so bad, that his heart would serve him to enter into one foot.

When Pharao the King of Egypt bought up, in the dear years, all the lands that were in every man's hand, so that all the people were fain to sell their inheritance for hunger; yet, idolater as he was, he would never suffer, for any need, the possessions of the priests to be sold, but made provision for them beside, and suffered them to keep their lands still, as the Bible beareth witness. And we verily trust that the good Christian princes of the Christian realm of England shall never fail of more favour toward the clergy of Christ, than had the prince idolater to the priests of his idols.[3]

MONASTIC ALMS.

I use not much myself to go very far abroad, and yet I see sometimes myself so many poor people at Westminster at the doles, of whom, as far as ever I heard, the monks use

---

[1] i.e., good for nothing.   [2] " Boystuouse."

[3] Supplication of Souls, Works, 303. This was written in 1529. Confiscation of monasteries by Henry VIII. in 1536-9.

not to send away many unserved, that myself for the press of them have been fain to ride another way. But one answered me to this once, and said that it was no thank to them, for it was land that good princes have given them. But as I then told him again, it were then much less thank to them that would now give good princes evil counsel for to take it from them. And also—if we call it no giving of alms by them, because the lands whereof they give it other good men have given them—whereof will you have them give alms, for they have none other?[1]

FEET-WASHING ON SHERE-THURSDAY.

Noble princes and great estates use that godly ceremony very religiously; and none (I suppose) nowhere more godly than our sovereign lord the king's grace here of this realm, both in humble manner washing and wiping, and kissing also, many poor folks' feet, after the number of the years of his age, and with right liberal and princely alms therewith.[2]

PAROCHIAL MATINS.

Some of us laymen think it a pain once in a week to rise so soon from sleep, and some to tarry so long fasting, as on the Sunday to come and hear out their matins. And yet is not the matins in every parish, neither all thing so early begun nor fully so long in doing, as it is in the Charter-house.[3]

LUTHERAN DEVOTION.

In many places in Almayne among their holy sects, where they were in the beginning wonderful hot upon sermons, they be now, blessed be God, waxen cold enough.

[1] *Apology*, Works, 895.   [2] *Treatise on the Passion*, Works, 1319.
[3] *Apology*, ch. xxix., Works, 894.

First in many places they sang the service in their mother tongue, men and women all, and there was a pretty sport for them for awhile. But after a little use thereof the pleasure of the novelty passed, and they set somewhat less thereby than by a gleeman's song. They changed also the mass, and soon after that many cast it up clean. Then was all their lust laid upon preaching, specially because every man might preach that would, saying that they followed the counsel of St. Paul, while one would bid the preacher hold his peace and let him speak another while, affirming that the spirit had revealed him the right sense, and that the preacher lied. Then turned they sermons in brawlings, so that sometimes the people parted them from pointing their preaching with fists. But now, as I hear say, the matter is well amended, for they can suffer one to preach as long as it please him, and no man once interrupt him ; for they be there waxen, women and all, so cunning that scantly come any to hear him.[1]

FRIAR FRAPPE.

He that looketh on this [*i.e.*, their manner of life], and then seeth them come forth and speak so holily, would he not ween that it were a sort[2] of friars following an "abbot of misrule" in a Christmas game that were pricked[3] in blankets, and then should stand by and preach upon a stool and make a mowing sermon?[4] And as lewd sermons as they make in such naughty games, would God that these men's earnest sermons were not yet much worse. But surely, as evil as the other be, yet is there more harm and more

---

[1] *Answer to Tindale*, Works, 398. [2] Company. [3] Dressed.
[4] Mocking.

deadly poison, too, in this one sermon of Tindale's than in a hundred sermons of Friar Frappe, that first gapeth and then blesseth, and looketh holily and preacheth ribaldry to the people that stand about. For there is not the worst thing that Friar Frappe preacheth in a lewd sport but father Tindale here writeth much worse in very great earnest, and much worse than doth the other abuseth the Scripture unto it. The other [F. Frappe], when he preacheth that men may lawfully go to lechery, he maketh commonly some sound texts of his own head, and dare not in such mad matters meddle with the very Scripture itself. But Tindale teacheth us in good earnest that friars may walk out and wed nuns, and is neither afraid nor ashamed to draw the Holy Scripture of God unto the maintenance of abominable sin and service of the devil. The other ribald in his fond sermon meddleth but with fleshly vices and worldly wantonness. But Tindale here, with an earnest high profession of godly spiritual doctrine, teacheth us a false faith and many mortal heresies; and would with Scripture destroy the Scripture, and amidst his earnest holiness falleth into mocks and mows, and maketh mad apish jesting against the holy ceremonies and blessed sacraments of the Saviour Christ, and the things sanctified with the blessed blood of our Saviour, Tindale turneth into scorn. Never was there any scoffing Friar Frappe, preaching upon a stool, that durst play the knavish fool on such a fashion as ye shall see Tindale do here. For if any should, his audience (were they never so wanton) would yet, at such words, if any spark of Christian zeal remained in their hearts, pull down the ribald by the skirt, and break the stool upon his head.[1]

[1] *Conf. of Tindale*, Works, 358.

IRRELIGION AND SUPERSTITION.

Some have I seen even in their last sickness set up in their death-bed, underpropped with pillows, take their play-fellows to them, and comfort themselves with cards, and this (they said) did ease them well to put phantasies out of their heads : and what phantasies, trow you? Such as I told you right now, of their own lewd life and peril of their soul, of heaven and of hell that irked them to think of, and therefore cast it out with card-play as long as ever they might, till the pure pangs of death pulled their heart from their play, and put them in a case they could not reckon their game. And then left them their gameners[1] and slily slunk away; and long was it not ere they gasped up the ghost. And what game they then came to, God knoweth and not I.

And many a fond fool there is that, when he lieth sick, will meddle with no physic in no manner wise, but send his cap or his hose to a wise woman, otherwise called a witch. Then sendeth she word again, that she hath spied in his hose where, when he took no heed, he was taken with a sprite between two doors as he went in the twilight, but the sprite would not let him feel it in five days after; and it hath all the while festered in his body, and that is the grief that paineth him so sore. But let him go to no leechcraft, nor any manner of physic, other than good meat and strong drink, for syrups should souse him up. But he shall have five leaves of valerian that she enchanted with a charm, and gathered with her left hand : let him lay those five leaves to his right thumb, not bind it fast to, but let it hang loose thereat by a green thread; he shall never need to change

[1] The companions of their game forsook them.

it, look it fall not away, but let it hang till be he whole, and
he shall need no more.   In such wise witches, and in such
mad medicines have many fools more faith a great deal than
in God.[1]

APOSTATES.

Bid him not pray for us till he put off his friar's coat, and
put on his frieze coat, and run out of his order, and catch
him a quean and call her his wife (618. A).   Lechery between friars and nuns they call it matrimony, but shall
have hell for the patrimony (621. A).   No Francis-friar bid
any bead[2] for us in his friar's coat, till he do off his grey
garments and clothe himself comely in grey Kendall-green
(618. F).   He fareth as he were from a friar waxen a fiddler,
and would at a tavern go get him a penny for a fit of mirth
(735. D).

BIBLE ABUSE.

Though the Bible were not taken to every lewd lad in his
own hand, to read a little rude lie when he list, and then
cast the book at his heels, or among other such as himself,
to keep a Quodlibet, and a pot-parliament thereon (246. B).

CHILDREN'S GAMES.

Take them as little babes untaught, and give them fair
words and pretty proper gear, rattles and cockbells and gay
golden shoes (366. F).   Such pretty plays as children be
wont to play, as cherry stone, marrow bone, " bokle pit,"
spurne-point, cobnut or " quayling " (574. F).   As children
make castles of tile-shards, and then make them their pastime in the throwing down again (1131. C).

---

[1] *Dialogue of Comfort*, Works, 1162.   [2] Say any prayer.

GAMESTERS.

They that go now full fresh in their guarded hosen, in their gay golden riven shirts, and in their silken sleeves, that nought have to bear it out but gaming, will once (I warrant you) fall from gaming to stealing, and start straight out of silk into hemp (952. H).

BEGGARS.

But as for the botch of his cankered heresies, without any clout or plaster he layeth out abroad to show, to beg withal among the blessed brethren, as beggars lay their sore legs out in sight. that lie a-begging a-Fridays about St. Saviour, and at the Savoy-gate (1076. F).

JUGGLERS.

As a juggler layeth forth his trinclets upon the table, and biddeth men look on this and look on that, and blow in his hand, and then, with certain strange words to make men muse, whirleth his juggling-stick about his fingers, while he playeth a false cast, and conveyeth, with the other hand, something slily into his purse or sleeve, or somewhere out of sight ; so, etc., etc. (1094. D).

TAVERN SIGNS.

I would wot what he[1] meaneth by sure tokens ; whether he mean only tokens and signs whereby we may conjecture that some of the Church be therein, though we know not which they be, as we may by a sign of a green garland perceive that there is wine in the house, though we know not whereabout the cellar is ; or else that we may so surely

---

[1] Barns.

know it that we cannot be deceived therein, as we be sure by the smoke and the sparkles that there is fire in the chimney (757. G).

DRUNKENNESS.

Some will eat salt meat purposely to give them a courage to the cup (1047. D).

So dowsy drunk that he could neither stand nor reel, but fell down sow-drunk in the mire (332. A).

BABIES SWATHED.

Died in their swaddling-clouts (263. G).

USE OF FLOWERS.

The manner then was in that country[1] to anoint the dead corpse with sweet odours, as we dress the winding-sheet with sweet herbs and flowers (1303. B).

ENGLISH BOOKS.

The very best way were neither to read this [More's answer to the heretics] nor theirs. but rather the people unlearned to occupy themselves in prayer, good meditation, and reading of such English books as most may nourish and increase devotion (of which kind is *Bonaventure of the Life of Christ, Gerson of the Following of Christ,* and the devout contemplative book of *Scala Perfectionis,*[2] with such other like) than in the learning what may well be answered unto heretics (356. D).

JUDGES AND JURIES.

In good faith I never saw the day yet but that I durst as well trust the truth of one judge as of two juries. But the

---

[1] In Palestine, in the time of our Lord.　　[2] By Hilton.

judges be so wise men, that for the avoiding of obloquy they will not be put in the trust (909. B).[1]

THE SCOTS.

After the rude rhymeless running of a Scottish jest (739. B). As for victuals, they may provide at home, and bring with them in bags and bottles, every man for three days at the least, as the Scots do for a skirmish (778. G).

STAGE PLAYS.

No Soudan in a stage play may make more bragging boasts, nor run out into more frantic rages (777. C).

CLERICAL DRESS.

For aught that I can see, a great part of the proud and pompous apparel that many priests, in years not long past, were by the pride and oversight of some few forced in a manner against their own wills to wear, was much more, I trow, than the one half spent and in manner well worn out (892. B).[2]

EDWARD IV.

By God's Blessed Lady! that was ever his oath (39. E).

Albeit, all the time of his reign he was with the people so

---

[1] Sir Thomas (989. G, 59) defends and explains this. He is not depreciating juries but praising judges: "I will say yet a little further, and I ween I shall not say so alone. I suppose verily that there be very few, but that so it might make a final end in their matter, would rather be content to put it whole into the judges' hands than trouble the country with calling up of the juries" (990. A). More was to experience that neither judges nor juries could be trusted against the king.

[2] Written in 1533.

benign, courteous, and so familiar, that no part of his virtues was more esteemed ; yet that condition in the end of his days—in which many princes, by a long-continued sovereignty, decline into a proud port from debonnair behaviour of their beginning—marvellously in him grew and increased (36. C).

He had left all gathering of money, which is the only thing that withdraweth the hearts of Englishmen from the prince (36. B).

PART THE FOURTH.

FANCIES, SPORTS, AND MERRY TALES.

They reprove me that I bring in, among the most earnest matters, fancies and sports and merry tales. But, as Horace sayeth, a man may sometimes say full sooth in game. And one that is but a layman, as I am, it may better haply become him merrily to tell his mind, than seriously and solemnly to preach. And, over this, I can scant believe that the brethren find any mirth in my books, for I have not much heard that they very merrily read them.[1]

CLIFF THE FOOL.

[More says that to lay to him as a fault, that he blames another man's book for causing divisions between the clergy and laity, although he himself cannot heal those divisions, is like saying that we must not blame a man for burning down a house, unless we can build it up again.]

" He putteth me in remembrance of an answer that a man of mine made once much after the same fashion. I had sometime one with me called Cliff—a man as well known as Master Henry Patenson. This Cliff had been many years mad, but age had taken from him the rage, so that he was meetly well waxen harmless among folk. Into Cliff's head came there sometimes in his madness such imaginations against images as these heretics have in their sadness. For like as some of them, which afterwards fled and ran away, and some fell to theft and were caught, pulled

[1] *Apology*, Works, 927.

(183)

down of late upon London Bridge the image of the Blessed
Martyr St. Thomas, so Cliff upon the same bridge upon a
time fell in talking unto an image of our Blessed Lady, and
after such blasphemies as the devil put then into his mouth
(and now-a-days bloweth out by the mouths of many
heretics, which, seem they never so sad, be yet more mad
than he) he set hand upon the child in her arm and there
brake off the neck.   And afterwards, when honest men,
dwellers upon the bridge, came home to mine house, and
there blamed Cliff before me, and asked him wherefore he
brake off the child's neck in our Lady's arm; when Cliff
had heard them he began to look well and earnestly upon
them, and like a man of sadness and gravity, he asked
them : ' Tell me this among you, there, have you not yet
set on his head again ?'   ' No (quoth they), we cannot.'
' No? (quoth Cliff), by the mass it is the more shame for
you.   Why speak you to me of it then ?' "

And even thus answereth me now this good man, which
where his seditious " Some says " set forth division, and
break the child's neck, reckoneth it a shame for me to find
any fault with him for the breaking, but if myself could
glue it together again.[1]

Crime the Mustard Maker.

Finally in the very end, to show that he could write, not
only in prose, he endeth all the whole book in this wise,
with a glorious rhyme :—

And thus the glorious Trinity
Have in His keeping both thee and me,

and maketh prayer for no more than but for them two, after

[1] *Debel. of Salem*, Works, 935.

the manner of the good man Grime, a mustard maker in
Cambridge, that was wont to pray for himself and his wife
and his child, and grace to make good mustard, and no
more.[1]

THE GALLANT AND THE FRIAR.

When a lewd gallant saw a poor friar going barefoot in a
great frost and snow, he asked him why he did take such
pain. And he answered that it was very little pain, if a man
would remember hell. "Yea, friar (quoth the gallant), but
what and there be none hell? Then art thou a great fool."
"Yea, master (quoth the friar), but what and there be hell?
Then is your mastership a much more fool."[2]

A WOMAN'S RETORT.

If I durst be bold to tell so sad a man a merry tale, I
would tell him of the friar that as he was preaching in the
country spied a poor wife of the parish whispering with her
pewfellow, and he, falling angry thereto, cried out unto her
aloud: "Hold thy babble, I bid thee, thou wife in the red
hood!" Which, when the housewife heard, she waxed as
angry again, and suddenly she started up and cried out
unto the friar again, that all the church rang thereon:
"Marry, sir, I beshrew his heart that babbleth most of us
both, for I do but whisper a word with my neighbour here
and thou hast babbled there all this hour ".[3]

A STRANGE SURETY.

A man came to a king and complained how sore he
feared that such a servant of his would kill him. And the

---

[1] *Debel. of Salem*, Works, 933.   [2] *Sup. of Souls*, Works, 329.
[3] *Debel. of Salem*, Works, 948.

king bade him : " Fear not, fellow, for I promise thee if he
kill thee he shall be hanged within a little while after ".
" Nay, my liege lord," quoth the poor soul, " I beseech
your grace let him be banged for it a great while afore.   For
I shall never live in the less fear till I see him hanged
first." [1]

THE MAID AND THE TILER.

[Tindale affirmed that those commonly called Catholics were the
real heretics, and those commonly called heretics the real Catholics ;
and when asked how this was to be proved, he replied that
heretics were those who held false doctrines as Catholics do.   Sir
Thomas replied.]

Now giveth forth Tindale such a counsel, as if one that
could no good skill of money, and were set to be a receiver,
would ask him counsel how he should do to be sure always
to take good money ; and Tindale would advise him to see
well that he took no bad.

And then, if he said again : " Yea, Master Tindale, but
I pray you teach me, then, how I may be sure that I take
no bad ".   " Marry ! (would Tindale say again) for that
shall I teach thee a way sure enough, that never shall
deceive thee, if thou do as I bid thee."   " What is that, I
pray you ? "   " Marry, look in any wise that thou take none
but good."

Such a good lesson, lo, did the tiler once teach the maid,
how she should bear home water in a sieve and spill never
a drop.   And when she brought the sieve to the water to
him to learn it, he bade her do no more but, ere ever she
put in the water, stop fast all the holes.

And then the maid laughed, and said that she could yet

<hr>

[1] *Debel. of Salem*, Works, 971.

teach him a thing that a man of his craft had more need to learn. For she could teach him how he should never fall, climbed he never so high, although men took away the ladder from him. And when he longed to learn that point to save his neck with, she bade him do no more but ever see surely to one thing, that is to wit, that for any haste he never come down faster than he went up.[1]

Luther's Marriage.

As the poor ploughman said unto the taverner that gave him water instead of wine : " God thank you, master winer, for your good wine, but in good faith, saving for the worshipful name of wine, I'd as lieve a drunken water " ; surely so may we well say to these new holy, spiritual married monks and friars, saving for the worshipful name of wedlock, it were as good they lived in lechery.[2]

Limited Faith.

When the friar apposed him in confession whether he meddled anything in witchcraft or necromancy, or had any belief in the devil, he answered him *Credere en le diable, mysir, no. Io grand fatige a credere in dio.* " Believe in the devil (quoth he), nay, nay, for I have work enough to believe in God, I." And so would I ween that you were far from all believing in the devil, ye have so much work to believe in God Himself, that ye be loth methink to meddle much in His saints.[3]

Destiny.

One of their sect in a good town in Almain, when he had robbed a man, and was brought before the judges, he could

---

[1] *Conf. of Tindale*, Works, 652.   [2] *Ibid.*, Works, 395.
[3] *Dialogue*, Works, 197.

not deny the deed, but he said it was his destiny to do it,
and therefore they might not blame him. They answered
him after his own doctrine, it was also their destiny to hang
him, and therefore he must as well hold them excused.[1]

SANDWICH HAVEN AND TENTERDEN STEEPLE.

In this opinion is Luther and his followers that it is not
lawful to any Christian man to fight against the Turk or to
make against him any resistance, though he come into
Christendom with a great army and labour to destroy all.
And unto this they lay that since the time that Christian
men first fell to fighting, it hath never increased but always
minished and decayed. . . . They fare as did an old sage
father fool in Kent, at such time as divers men of worship
assembled old folk of the country to devise about the amendment of Sandwich haven. At which time they began first
to ensearch by reason and by the report of old men there-
about, what thing had been the occasion that so good a
haven was in so few years so sore decayed and such sands
risen, and such shallow flats made therewith, that right
small vessels had now much work to come in at divers
tides, where great ships were, within few years past, accustomed to ride without difficulty. And some laying the fault
to Goodwin Sands, some to the lands inned [enclosed] by
divers owners in the Isle of Thanet, out of the channel in
which the sea was wont to compass the isle and bring the
vessels round about it, whose course at the ebb was wont to
scour the haven, which now, the sea [being] excluded thence,
for lack of such course and scouring, is choked up with
sand. As they thus alledged, divers with divers causes,

[1] *Dialogue*, Works, 274.

there started up one good old father and said: "Yea,
masters, say every man what he will, cha [I've] marked this
matter well as some other; and by God I wot how it waxed
naught well enough.   For I knew it good, and have marked,
so chave [so I have], when it began to wax worse."   "And
what hath hurt it, good father?" quoth the gentlemen.
"By my faith, masters (quoth he), yonder same Tenterden
steeple and nothing else; that, by the mass cholde [I would]
it were a fair fish-pole."   "Why hath the steeple hurt the
haven, good father?" quoth they.   "Nay, by'r Lady,
masters (quoth he), yche [I] cannot tell you well why, but
chote [I wot] well it hath.   For by God I knew it a good
haven till that steeple was builded, and by the Mary-mass
cha [I've] marked it well, it never throve since."

And thus wisely spake these holy Lutherans, which,
sowing schisms and factions among Christian people, lay
the loss thereof in the withstanding of the Turk's invasion,
and the resisting of his malice.[1]

THE SULTAN OF SYRIA.

You should find him as shamefast as a friend of mine (a
merchant) found once the Soudan of Syria, to whom (being
certain years about his merchandise in that country) he gave
a great sum of money for a certain office meet for him
there for the while, which he scant had him granted and
put in his hand, but that, ere ever it were worth ought
unto him, the Soudan suddenly sold it to another of his own
sect, and put our Hungarian out.   Then came he to him,
and humbly put him in remembrance of his grant passed his
own mouth and signed with his own hand.   Whereunto the

---

[1] *Dialogue*, Works, 277.

Soudan answered him with a grim countenance: "I will thou wit it, losel, that neither my mouth nor my hand shall be master over me, to bind all my body at their pleasure, but I will so be lord and master over them both, that whatsoever the one say, or the other write, I will be at mine own liberty to do what me list myself, and ask them both no leave.   And therefore go get thee hence out of my countries, knave." [1]

The Carver's Wife.

When a carver told his wife that he would, upon a Good Friday, needs have killed himself for Christ's sake, as Christ was killed for him, she would not in vain plead against his mind, but well and wisely put him in remembrance, that if he would die for Christ as Christ died for him, it were then convenient for him to die even after the same fashion.   And that might not be by his own hands, but by the hand of some other : for Christ, pardie, killed not Himself.   And because her husband should need to make no more of counsel (for that would he not in no wise) she offered him, that for God's sake she would secretly herself crucify him on a great cross, that he had made to nail a new carved crucifix upon.   Whereof when he was very glad, yet she bethought her, that Christ was bounden to a pillar and beaten first, and after crowned with thorns.   Whereupon when she had (by his own assent) bound him fast to a post, she left not heating, with holy exhortation to suffer so much and so long, that ere ever she left work and unbound him, praying him nevertheless that she might put on his head, and drive it well down, a crown of thorns that she

[1] *Dialogue of Comfort*, Works, 1229.

had writhen for him and brought him : he said, he thought this was enough for that year ; he would pray God to for-bear him of the remainder till Good Friday come again. But when it came again the next year, then was his lust past ; he longed to follow Christ no farther.[1]

WORD-JUGGLING.

Likewise, as though a sophister would, with a fond argument, prove unto a simple soul that two eggs were three, because that "*there* is one, and *there* be twain, and one and twain make three"; the simple, unlearned man, though he lack learning to soyle [refute] his fond argument, hath yet wit enough to laugh thereat, and to eat the two eggs himself, and bid the sophister take and eat the third ; so is every faithful man as sure in the sight of his soul, how apparently soever a heretic argue by Scripture to the contrary, that the common faith of Christ's Catholic Church is out of question true, and that the Scripture understanden right is never thereto contrary.[2]

ANOTHER EXAMPLE.

If he mean to read his riddle on this fashion, then he soyleth his strange riddle as bluntly as an old wife of Culnaw did once among scholars of Oxenford that sojourned with her for death [in the time of the plague]. Which, while they were on a time for their sport purposing riddles among them, she began to put forth one of hers too, and said : " Aread my riddle, what is that ? I knew one that shot at a hart and killed a haddock." And when we had

[1] *Dialogue of Comfort*, Works, 1193.
[2] *Conf. of Tindale*, Works, 475.

everybody much mused how that might be, and then prayed
her to declare her riddle herself, after long request she said
at the last that there was once a fisher that came aland in
a place where he saw a hart and shot thereat, but he hit
it not ; and afterwards he went again to the sea and caught
a haddock and killed it.[1]

ANOTHER EXAMPLE.

Tindale here by the name of faith understands hope and
trust in God, as he juggleth continually with that word, for
such equivocations and divers understandings of one word
serve him for his goblets, his galls, and his juggling-stick, in
all the proper points of his whole conveyance and his
legerdemain.[2]

ORIGEN.

I have divers good and honest witnesses to bring forth
when time requireth—St. Austin, St. Jerome, St. Cyprian,
St. Chrysostom, and a great many more—which have also
testified for my part in this matter more than a thousand
years ago. Yet have I another ancient sad father also, one
that they call Origen. And when I desired him to come
and bear witness with me in this matter, he seemed at the
first very well content. But when I told him that he should
meet with Tindale, he blessed himself and shrank back,
and said he had liever go some other way many a mile than
once meddle with him. "For I shall tell you, sir," quoth he,
"before this time a right honourable man, very cunning and
yet more virtuous, the good Bishop of Rochester, in a great
audience, brought me in for a witness against Luther even
in this same matter, about the time of Tindale's evil

---

[1] *Conf. of Tindale*, Works, 552.   [2] *Ibid.*, Works, 572.

translated Testament. But Tindale, as soon as he heard of my name, without any respect of honesty fell in a rage with me, and all too rated me, and called me stark heretic, and that the starkest that ever was." This tale Origen told me, and swore by St. Simkin that he was never so said unto of such a lewd fellow since he was first born of his mother, and therefore he would never meddle with Tindale more. Now, indeed, it was not well done of Tindale to leave reasoning and fall a-scolding, chiding and brawling as if he were a bawdy beggar of Billiter Lane. Fie, for shame! he should have favoured and forborne him somewhat, and it had been but for his age. For Origen is now thirteen hundred years old or thereabouts, and this was not much above seven years since.[1]

DAVY THE DUTCHMAN.

He made me remember a like matter of a man of mine done seven year afore, one Davy, a Dutchman, which had been married in England, and saying that his wife was dead and buried at Worcester two years before, while he was in his country, and giving her much praise, and often telling us how sorry he was when he came home and found her dead, and how heavily he had made her bitter prayers at her grave, went about, while he waited upon me at Bruges in the king's business, to marry there an honest widow's daughter. And so happed it that, even upon the day when they should have been made handfast and ensured together, was I advertised from London by my wife's letter that Davy's wife was alive, and had been at my house to seek him. Whereupon I called him before me and others, and read the letter to him. " Marry, master,"

[1] *Conf. of Tindale,* Works, 410.

quoth he, " that letter saith, methink, that my wife is alive."
" Yea, beast," quoth I, " that she is."   " Marry," quoth he,
" then I am well apaid, for she is a good woman."   " Yea,"
quoth I, " but why art thou such a naughty, wretched man,
that thou wouldest here wed another?   Didst thou not
say she was dead?"   " Yes, marry," quoth he, " men of
Worcester told me so."   " Why," quoth I, " thou false
beast, didst thou not tell me and all my house that thou
wert at her grave thyself?"   " Yea, marry, master," quoth
he, " so I was, but I could not look in, ye wot well." [1]

Paterson's Proclamation.

They that tell us that we shall be damned but if we
believe right, and then tell us that we cannot know that but
by the Scripture, and that the Scripture cannot be so learned
but of a true teacher, and they tell us we cannot be sure
of a true teacher, and so cannot be sure to understand
it right, and yet say that God will damn us for understanding it wrong, or not understanding at all; they that thus
tell us put me in mind of a tale that they tell of Master
Henry Paterson, a man of known wisdom in London and
almost everywhere else.   Which when he waited once on
his master in the emperor's court at Bruges, and was
there soon perceived upon the sight for a man of special
wit by himself, and unlike the common sort, they caught a
sport in angering of him, and out of divers corners hurled
at him such things as angered him and hurt him not.
Thereupon he gathered up good stones, not gunstones but
as hard as they, and those he put apace into his bosom,
and then stood him up upon a bench, and made a procla-

---

[1] *Conf. of Tindale*, Works, 728.

mation aloud that every man might hear him, in which he commanded every man upon their own perils to depart, except only those that hurled at him, to the intent that he might know them and hurl at them again, and hurt none other body but his enemies ; but whosoever tarried after his proclamation made he would take him for one of the hurlers, or else for one of their counsellors, and then have at their heads, whosoever they were that would abide.

Now was his proclamation in English, and the company that heard him were such as understood none, but stood still and gaped upon him and laughed at him. And by-and-by one hurled at him again ; and anon, as he saw that : "What, whoresons (quoth he), ye stand still every one I ween, and not one of you will remove a foot for all my proclamations, and thereby I see well ye be hurlers, or of counsel with the hurlers, all the whole many of you, and therefore have at you all again ". And with the word he hurled a great stone out at adventure among them, he neither wist nor sought[1] at whom, but lighted upon a Burgundian's head and brake his pate that the blood ran about his ears ; and Master Henry bade him stand to his harms hardily, for why would he not beware then, and get him thence betime, when he gave him before so great courteous warning.[2]

"PLAY THE GOOD COMPANION."

[Margaret Roper writes as follows :—]

As far as I can call to mind, my father's tale was this, that there is a court belonging unto every fair, to do justice in such things as happen within the same. Upon a

---

[1] Cared. [2] *Conf. of Tindale*, Works, 767.

time at such a court holden at Bartylmewe [1] Fair there was
an escheator of London that had arrested a man that was
outlawed, and had seized his goods that he had brought
into the fair, tolling him out of the fair by a train.[2] The
man that was arrested (and his goods seized) was a northern
man, which by his friends made the escheator within the
fair to be arrested upon an action (I wot ne'er what). And
so was he brought before the judge of the court, and at the
last the matter came to a certain ceremony to be tried by a
quest of twelve men, a jury as I remember they call it, or
else a perjury. Now had the clothman, by friendship of
the officers, found the means to have all the quest almost
made of the northern men, such as had their booths there
standing in the fair. Now was it come to the last day in
the afternoon, and the twelve men had heard both the
parties and their counsel tell their tales at the bar, and were
from the bar had into a place to talk and commune and
agree upon their verdict. They were scant come in together but the northern men were agreed, and in effect all
the other too, to cast our London escheator. They thought
there needed no more to prove that he did wrong, than
even the name of his bare office alone.

But then was there among them, as the devil would, an
honest man of another quarter, that was called Company.
And because the fellow seemed but a fool, and sat still and
said nothing, they made no reckoning of him, but said:
"We be agreed now ; come and let us go give our verdict".
Then when the poor fellow saw that they made such haste,
and his mind nothing gave him that way that theirs did (if
their minds gave them that way that they said), he prayed

---

[1] St. Bartholomew's Fair.   ·   [2] Stratagem.

them to tarry and talk upon the matter, and tell him such reason therein that he might think as they did; and when he so should do he would be glad to say with them, or else (he said) they must pardon him. For since he had a soul of his own to keep as they had, he must say as he thought for his, as they must for theirs.

. When they heard this they were half angry with him: "What! good fellow (quoth one of the northern men), where wons[1] thou? Be not we eleven here, and thou but one, lo! alone,[2] and all we be agreed? Whereto shouldst thou stick? What is thy name, good fellow?" "Masters (quoth he), my name is called Company." "Company! (quoth they), now by thy troth, good fellow, play then the good companion; come therein forth with us and pass even for good company." "Would God, good masters (quoth the man again), that there lay no more weight thereon. But now, when we shall hence and come before God, and that He shall send you to heaven for doing according to your conscience, and me to the devil for doing against mine, in passing at your request here for good company now—by God, Master Dickinson (that was one of the northern men's names), if I shall then say to all you again: 'Masters, I went once for good company with you, which is the cause that I go now to hell; play you the good fellows now again with me. As I went then for good company with you, so some of you go now for good company with me.' Would you go, Master Dickinson? Nay, nay, by our Lady; nor never one of you all. And, therefore, must ye pardon me

[1] Livest.

[2] It is given in the northern dialect: "Be not we eleven here and thou ne but ene, la! alene," etc.

from passing as you pass ; but if I thought in the matter as you do, I dare not in such a matter pass for good company."

And when my father had told me this tale, then said he further thus : " I pray thee, now, good Margaret, tell me this, wouldest thou wish thy poor father, being at the least wise somewhat learned, less to regard the peril of his soul than did there that honest, unlearned man ? I meddle not (you wot well) with conscience of any man that hath sworn, nor I take not upon me to be their judge. But now, if they do well, and that their conscience grudge them not ; if I— with my conscience to the contrary—should, for good company, pass as with them and swear as they do, when all our souls hereafter shall pass out of this world and stand in judgment at the bar before the high Judge, if He judge them to heaven and me to the devil, because I did as they did, not thinking as they thought, if I should then say (as the good man Company said) : ' Mine old good lords and friends—naming such a lord and such, yea, and some bishops, peradventure, of such as I love best—I sware because you sware, and went that way that you went ; do likewise for me now ; let me not go alone if there be any good fellowship with you, some of you come with me '. By my troth, Margaret, I may say to thee in secret counsel here between us twain (let it go no further, I beseech thee, heartily), I find the friendship of this wretched world so fickle, that for anything that I could treat or pray, that would for good fellowship go to the devil with me, among them all, I ween, I should not find one." [1]

[1] Works, 1437.

A Strange Temptation.

Some of my folk here can tell you that even yesterday one that came out of Vienna showed us, among other talking, that a rich widow (but I forgot to ask where it happed), having all her life a high, proud mind and a fell, as those two virtues are wont always to keep company together, was at debate with another neighbour of hers in the town, and on a time she made of her counsel a poor neighbour of hers, whom she thought for money she might induce to follow her mind.   With him secretly she brake, and offered him ten ducats for his labour, to do so much for her as in a morning early to come to her house, and with an axe, unknown privily, to strike off her head.   And when he had so done, then convey the bloody axe into the house of him with whom she was at debate, in some such manner wise as it might be thought that he had murdered her for malice, and then she thought she should be taken for a martyr.   And yet had she further devised, that another sum of money should after be sent to Rome, and that there should be means made to the Pope that she might in all haste be canonised.   This poor man promised, but intended not to perform it.   Howbeit, when he deferred it, she provided the axe herself, and he appointed with her the morning when he should come and do it.   But then set he such other folk, as he would should know her frantic phantasy, in such place appointed as they might well hear her and him talk together.   And after that he had talked with her thereof what he would, so much as he thought was enough, he made her lie down, and took up the axe in his one hand, and with the other hand he felt the edge, and found a fault that it was not sharp, and that, therefore, he would in no wise do it till that he had ground it sharp ; he could not else (he said) for pity, it would put her to so much pain ; and so full sore against her will for that time she kept her head still. But because she would no more suffer any to deceive her so, and fode her forth with delays, ere it was very long after she hanged herself with her own hands.[1]

Fears of the Night.

Now consider further yet, that the prophet in the fore-remembered verses saith not, that in the night walk only the lions' whelps, but also, *omnes bestiæ sylvarum*, all the beasts of the wood. Now wot you well, that if a man walk through the wood in the night, many things may make him afraid, of which in the day he would not be afraid a whit, for in the night every bush to him that waxeth once afraid, seemeth a thief.

I remember that when I was a young man,[2] I was once in the war with the king, then my master (God assoil his soul !) and we were camped within the Turk's ground many a mile beyond Belgrade, which would God were ours now, as well as it was then ! But so happed it, that in our camp about midnight, there suddenly rose rumours that the Turk's whole army was secretly stealing upon us, wherewith our noble host was warned to arm them in haste, and set themself in array to fight. And then were scouts of ours that brought these sudden tidings, examined more leisurely by the council, what surety or what likelihood they had perceived therein. Of whom one showed, that by the glimmer-

---

[1] *Dialogue of Comfort*, Works, 1188.
[2] The speaker is supposed to be a Hungarian nobleman.

ing of the moon he had espied and perceived and seen them himself, coming on softly and soberly in a long range, all in good order, not one farther forth than the other in the fore-front, but as even as the thread, and in breadth farther than he could see in length.   His fellows being examined said that he was somewhat pricked forth before them, and came so fast back to tell it them that they thought it rather time to make haste and give warning to the camp, than to go nearer unto them : for they were not so far off, but that they had yet themself somewhat an imperfect sight of them too.   Thus stood we watching all the remnant of the night evermore hearkening when we should hear them come, with, "Hush, stand still, methink I hear a trampling"; so that at last many of us thought we heard them ourself also. But when the day was sprung, and that we saw no man, out was our scourer sent again, and some of our captains with him, to show them whereabout the place was in which he perceived them.   And when they came thither they found that great fearful army of the Turks so soberly coming on, turned (God be thanked!) into a fair long hedge, standing even stone still.

And thus fareth it in the night's fear of tribulation, in which the devil, to bear down and overwhelm with dread the faithful hope that we should have in God, casteth in our imagination much more fear than cause.   For while there walk in that night not only the lions' whelps, but over that all the beasts of the wood beside, the beast that we hear roar in the dark night of tribulation and fear it for a lion, we sometimes find well afterwards in the day, that it was no lion at all, but a silly rude roaring ass.[1]

[1] *Dialogue of Comfort*, Works, 1181.

A PROVOKING WIFE.

Antony.—There was here in Buda, in King Ladislaus'
days, a good, poor, honest man's wife : this woman was so
fiendish that the devil, perceiving her nature, put her in
the mind that she should anger her husband so sore, that
she might give him occasion to kill her, and then he should
be hanged for her.

Vincent.—This was a strange temptation indeed.   What
the devil should she be the better then ?

Antony.—Nothing but that it eased her shrewd stomach
before, to think that her husband should be hanged after.
And peradventure if you look about the world and consider
it well, you shall find more such stomachs than a few.
Have you never heard no furious body plainly say, that to
see some such man have a mischief, he would with good
will be content to lie as long in hell as God liveth in
heaven ?

Vincent.—Forsooth, and some such have I heard of.

Antony.—This mind of his was not much less mad than
hers, but rather haply the more mad of the twain :. for the
woman peradventure did not cast so far peril therein.   But
to tell you now to what good pass her charitable purpose
came : as her husband (the man was a carpenter) stood
hewing with his chip-axe upon a piece of timber, she began
after her old guise so to revile him, that the man waxed
wrath at last, and bade her get in or he would lay the helm
of his axe about her back, and said also, that it were little
sin even with that axe-head to chop off that unhappy head
of hers that carried such an ungracious tongue therein.   At
that word the devil took his time, and whetted her tongue

against her teeth, and when it was well sharped, she sware
to him in very fierce anger : " By the mass, I would thou
wouldst : here lieth my head, lo ! (and therewith down she
laid her head upon the same timber log) if thou smite it
not off, I beshrew thy heart ". With that, likewise, as the
devil stood at her elbow, so stood (as I heard say) his good
angel at his, and gave him ghostly courage, and bade him
be bold and do it. And so the good man up with his chip-
axe, and at a chop chopped off her head indeed. There
were standing other folk by, which had a good sport to
hear her chide, but little they looked for this chance, till it
was done ere they could let it. They said they heard her
tongue babble in her head, and call evil names twice after
the head was from the body. At the leastwise afterward
unto the king thus they reported all, except only one, and
that was a woman, and she said that she heard it not.

Vincent.—Forsooth, this was a wonderful work. What
became, Uncle, of the man ?

Antony.—The king gave him his pardon.

Vincent.—Verily he might in conscience do no less.

Antony.—But then was it farther almost at another
point, that there should have been a statute made, that in
such case there should never after pardon be granted, but,
the truth being able to be proved, no husband should need
any pardon, but should have leave by the law to follow the
sample of the carpenter, and do the same.

Vincent.—How happed it, Uncle, that the good law was
left unmade ?

Antony.—How happed it ? As it happeth, Cousin, that
many more be left unmade as well as it, and within a little
as good as it too, both here and in other countries ; and,

sometimes some worse made in their stead.   But (as they
say) the let of that law was the queen's grace, God forgive
her soul! it was the greatest thing, I ween, good lady, that
she had to answer for when she died, for surely, save for
that one thing, she was a full blessed woman.[1]

THE WOLF, THE ASS, AND THE FOX.

Antony.—My mother had, when I was a little boy, a good
old woman that took heed to her children ; they called her
Mother Maud : I trow, you have heard of her.

Vincent.—Yea, yea, very much. ·

Antony.—She was wont, when she sat by the fire with us,
to tell us that were children many childish tales.   I remember me that among other of her fond tales, she told us once,
that the ass and the wolf came on a time to confession to
the fox.   The poor ass came to shrift in the shrovetide, a
day or two before Ash Wednesday ; but the wolf would not
come to confession until he saw first Palm Sunday past, and
then foded yet forth farther until Good Friday.   The fox
asked the ass before he began *Benedicite*, wherefore he came
to confession so soon before Lent began.   The poor beast
answered him again : for fear of deadly sin if he should lose
his part of any of those prayers that the priest in the clean-
sing days prayeth for them that are confessed already.
Then in his shrift he had a marvellous grudge in his inward
conscience, that he had one day given his master a cause of
anger, in that, that with his rude roaring before his master
arose, he had awaked him out of his sleep, and bereaved
him out of his rest.   The fox for that fault, like a good
discreet confessor, charged him to do so no more, but lie
still and sleep like a good son himself, till his master were

[1] *Dialogue of Comfort*, Works, 1187.

up and ready to go to work, and so should he be sure, that he should not wake him no more.

To tell you all the poor ass's confession, it were a long work, for everything that he did was deadly sin with him, the poor soul was so scrupulous. But his wise wily confessor accounted them for trifles, as they were, and sware afterward unto the badger, that he was so weary to sit so long and hear him, that saving for the manners' sake, he had liever have sitten all the while at breakfast with a good fat goose. But when it came to the penance giving, the fox found that the most weighty sin in all his shrift was gluttony, and therefore he discreetly gave him in penance, that he should never for greediness of his own meat do any other beast any harm or hindrance, and then eat his meat, and study for no more.

Now, as good Mother Maud told us, when the wolf came to confession to Father Reynard (for that was, she said, the fox's name) upon Good Friday, his confessor shook his great pair of beads upon him almost as big as bowls, and asked him wherefore he came so late. " Forsooth, Father Reynard," quoth he, " I must needs tell you the truth : I come (you wot well) therefor, I durst come no sooner, for fear lest you would for any gluttony have given me in penance to fast some part of this Lent." " Nay, nay," quoth Father Fox, " I am not so unreasonable : for I fast none of it myself. For I may say to thee, son, between us twain here in confession, it is no commandment of God this fasting, but an invention of man. The priests make folk fast and put them to pain about the moonshine in the water, and do but make folk fools : but they shall make me no such fool, I warrant thee, son. For I eat flesh all this

Lent, myself I. Howbeit, indeed, because I will not be occasion of slander, I therefore eat it secretly in my chamber, out of sight of all such foolish brethren as for their weak scrupulous conscience would wax offended withal, and so would I counsel you to do." "Forsooth, Father Fox," quoth the wolf, "and so I thank God I do, so near as I can. For when I go to my meat, I take none other company with me, but such sure brethren as are of mine own nature, whose consciences are not weak, I warrant you, but their stomachs as strong as mine." "Well, then, no matter," quoth Father Fox.

But when he heard after by his confession, that he was so great a ravener, that he devoured and spent sometime so much victual at one meal, as the price thereof would well find some poor man with his wife and children almost all the week; then he prudently reproved that point in him, and preached him a process of his own temperance, which never used, as he said, to pass upon himself the value of sixpence at a meal, no nor yet so much neither. "For when I bring home a goose," quoth he, "not out of the poulterer's shop, where folk find them out of their feathers ready plucked, and see which is the fattest and yet for sixpence buy and choose the best, but out of the housewife's house at the first hand, which may somewhat better cheap afford them, you wot well, than the poulterer may, nor yet cannot be suffered to see them plucked, and stand and choose them by day, but am fain by night to take at adventure, and when I come home, am fain to do the labour to pluck her myself: yet for all this, though it be but lean, and I ween not well worth a groat, serveth it me somewhat for all that, both dinner and supper too. And therefore, as

for that you live of raven, therein can I find no fault : you
have used it so long, that I think you can do none other.
And therefore were it folly to forbid it you, and (to say the
truth) against good conscience too.   For live you must, I
wot well, and other craft can you none ; and therefore, as
reason is, must you live by that.   But yet, you wot well,
too much is too much, and measure is a merry mean, which
I perceive by your shrift you have never used to keep.
And therefore, surely, this shall be your penance : that you
shall all this year now pass upon yourself the price of sixpence at a meal, as near as your conscience can guess the
price."

Their shrift have I showed you, as Mother Maud showed
it us.   But now serveth for our matter the conscience of
them both, in the true performing of their penance.   The
poor ass after his shrift, when he waxed a hungered, saw a
sow lie with her pigs well lapped in new straw, and near he
drew and thought to have eaten of the straw.   But anon
his scrupulous conscience began therein to grudge him.   For
while his penance was, that for greediness of his meat he
should do none other body harm ; he thought he might not
eat one straw thereof, lest for lack of that straw some of
those pigs might hap to die for cold.   So held he still his
hunger, till one brought him meat.   But when he should
fall thereto, then fell he yet in a far further scruple ; for
then it came in his mind that he should yet break his
penance, if he should eat any of that either, since he was
commanded by his ghostly father, that he should not for
his own meat hinder any other beast.   For he thought, that
if he eat not that meat, some other beast might hap to have
it, and so should he by the eating of it peradventure hinder

another.   And thus stood he still fasting, till when he told
the cause, his ghostly father came and informed him better,
and then he cast off that scruple, and fell mannerly to his
meat, and was a right honest ass many a fair day after.

Now this wolf had cast out in confession all his old raven,
and then hunger pricked him forward, that he should begin
all afresh.   But yet the prick of conscience withdrew and
held him back, because he would not for breaking of his
penance take any prey for his mealtide that should pass
the price of sixpence.   It happed him then as he walked
prowling for his gear about, he came where a man had in
few days before cast off two old, lean, and lame horses, so
sick, that no flesh was there left on them ; and the one,
when the wolf came by, could scant stand upon his legs,
and the other already dead, and his skin ripped off and
carried away.   And as he looked upon them suddenly, he
was first about to feed upon them, and whet his teeth on
their bones.   But as he looked aside, he spied a fair cow in
a close walking with her young calf by her side.   And as
soon as he saw them, his conscience began to grudge him
against both those two horses.   And then he sighed, and
said unto himself : " Alas ! wicked wretch that I am, I had
almost broken my penance ere I was ware.   For yonder
dead horse, because I never saw no dead horse sold in the
market, and I should even die therefore, I cannot devise
what price I should set upon him ; but in my conscience I
set him far above sixpence, and therefore I dare not meddle
with him.   Now, then, is yonder quick horse, of likelihood
worth a great deal of money : for horses be dear in this
country, specially such soft amblers ; for I see by his face
he trotteth not, nor can scant shift a foot.   And therefore I

may not meddle with him, for he very far passeth my sixpence.   But kine this country here hath enough, but money
have they very little ; and therefore, considering the plenty
of the kine, and the scarcity of the money, as for yonder
cow seemeth unto me in my conscience worth not past a
groat, an she be worth so much.   Now, then, as for her calf,
is not so much as she by half.   And therefore, while the
cow is in my conscience worth but fourpence, my conscience cannot serve me for sin of my soul to appraise her
calf above twopence, and so pass they not sixpence between
them both.   And therefore them twain may I well eat at
this one meal, and break not my penance at all."   And so
therefore he did, without any scruple of conscience.

If such beasts could speak now, as Mother Maud said
they could then, some of them would, I ween, tell a tale
almost as wise as this, wherein, save for the minishing of old
Mother Maud's tale, else would a shorter process have
served.   But yet, as peevish as the parable is, in this it
serveth for our purpose, that the fear of a conscience somewhat scrupulous, though it be painful and troublous to him
that hath it, like as this poor ass had here, is less harm yet,
than a conscience over large, or such as for his own fantasy
the man list to frame himself, now drawing it narrow, now
stretching it in breadth, after the manner of a cheverel point,
to serve on every side for his own commodity, as did here
the wily wolf.   But such folk are out of tribulation, and
comfort need they none, and therefore are they out of our
matter.   But those that are in the night's fear of their own
scrupulous conscience, let them be well ware, as I said, that
the devil, for weariness of the one, draw them not into the
other ; and while he would flee from Scylla, draw him into

14

Charybdis. He must do as doth a ship that should come
into an haven, in the mouth whereof lie secret rocks under the
water on both sides. If he be by mishap entered in among
them that are on the one side, and cannot tell how to get
out : he must get a substantial cunning pilot, that so can
conduct him from the rocks that are on that side, that yet
he bring him not into those that are on the other side, but
can guide him in the midway.[1]

TALKATIVE NUN AND TALKATIVE WIFE.

Antony.—Between you and me, it fared as it did once
between a nun and her brother. Very virtuous was this
lady, and of a very virtuous place, a close religion,[2] and
therein had been long, in all which time she had never seen
her brother, which was in like wise very virtuous, and had
been far off at an university, and had there taken the degree of doctor in divinity. When he was come home he
went to see his sister, as he that highly rejoiced in her
virtue. So came she to the grate that they call, I trow, the
locutory, and after their holy watch-word spoken on both
the sides, after the manner used in that place, the one took
the other by the tip of the finger (for hand would there be
none wrungen through the grate), and forthwith began my
lady to give her brother a sermon of the wretchedness of
this world, and the frailty of the flesh, and the subtle slights
of the wicked fiend, and gave him surely good counsel,
saving somewhat too long, how he should be well ware in
his living, and master well his body for saving of his soul ;
and yet, ere her own tale came all at an end, she began to
find a little fault with him, and said : " In good faith,

---

[1] *Dialogue of Comfort*, Works, 1183.   [2] Enclosed religious order.

Brother, I do somewhat marvel that you, that have been at
learning so long, and are doctor, and so learned in the law
of God, do not now at our meeting, while we meet so
seldom, to me that am your sister and a simple, unlearned
soul, give of your charity some fruitful exhortation. For I
doubt not but you can say some good thing yourself." "By
my troth, good Sister," quoth her brother, "I cannot for
you. For your tongue hath never ceased, but said enough
for us both." And so, Cousin, I remember, that when I
was once fallen in, I left you little space to say aught between. But now, will I, therefore, take another way with
you ; for I shall of our talking drive you to the one-half.

Vincent.—Now, forsooth, Uncle, this was a merry tale.
But now if you make me talk the one-half, then shall you be
contented far otherwise than there was of late a kinswoman
of your own, but which will I not tell you ; guess her an
you can. Her husband had much pleasure in the manner
and behaviour of another honest man, and kept him therefore much company ; by the reason whereof he was at his
mealtime the more oft from home. So happed it on a time
that his wife and he together dined or supped with that
neighbour of theirs, and then she made a merry quarrel to
him for making her husband so good cheer out a-door, that
she could not have him at home. "Forsooth, mistress,"
quoth he (as he was a dry merry man), "in my company
nothing keepeth him but one ; serve you him with the
same, and he will never be from you." "What gay thing
may that be ?" quoth our cousin then. "Forsooth, mistress," quoth he, "your husband loveth well to talk, and
when he sitteth with me, I let him have all the words." "All
the words !" quoth she. "Marry that I am content ; he

shall have all the words with a good will, as he hath ever
had. But I speak them all myself, and give them all to
him ; and for aught that I care for them, so he shall have
them still. But otherwise to say, that he shall have them
all, you shall keep them still, rather than he get the half." [1]

Love of Flattery.

Vincent.—When I was first in Almaine, Uncle, it happed
me to be somewhat favoured with a great man of the
church, and a great state, one of the greatest in all that
country there. [2]   And indeed whosoever might spend as
much as he might in one thing and other, were a right
great estate in any country of Christendom. But glorious
was he very far above all measure, and that was great pity,
for it did harm and made him abuse many great gifts that
God had given him. Never was he satiate of hearing his
own praise. So happed it one day, that he had in a great
audience made an oration in a certain manner, wherein he
liked himself so well, that at his dinner he sat on thorns,
till he might hear how they that sat with him at his board
would commend it. And when he had sitten musing a
while, devising (as I thought after) on some pretty proper
way to bring it in withal, at last, for lack of a better (lest
he should have letted the matter too long) he brought it
even bluntly forth, and asked us all that sat at his board's
end (for at his own mess in the midst there sat but himself
alone), how well we liked his oration that he had made that
day. But in faith, Uncle, when that problem was once proposed, till it was full answered, no man I ween ate one

[1] *Dialogue of Comfort*, Works, 1170.
[2] This story is generally supposed to apply to Cardinal Wolsey.

morsel of meat more : every man was fallen in so deep a study, for the fiuding of some exquisite praise. For he that should have brought out but a vulgar and common commendation would have thought himself shamed for ever.

Then said we our sentences by row as we sat, from the lowest unto the highest in good order, as it had been a great matter of the common weal in a right solemn council. When it came to my part (I will not say it for no boast, Uncle), methought, by our lady ! for my part I quit myself · pretty well. And I liked myself the better, because methought my words (being but a stranger) went yet with some grace in the Almaine tongue, wherein, letting my Latin alone, me listed to show my cunning. And I hoped to be liked the better, because I saw that he that sat next me, and should say his sentence after me, was an unlearned priest : for he could speak no Latin at all. But when he came forth for his part with my lord's commendation, the wily fox had been so well accustomed in court with the craft of flattery that he went beyond me too far. And then might I see by him, what excellency a right mean wit may come to in one craft, that in all his whole life studieth and busieth his wit about no more but that one. But I made after a solemn vow to myself, that if ever he and I were matched together at that board again, when we should fall to our flattery I would flatter in Latin, that he should not contend with me no more. For though I could be content to be outrun of a horse, yet would I no more abide it to be outrun of an ass. But, Uncle, here began now the game : he that sat highest, and was to speak the last, was a great beneficed man, and not a doctor only, but also somewhat learned indeed in the laws of the Church. A world it was

to see how he marked every man's word that spake before
him, and it seemed that every word, the more proper that it
was the worse he liked it, for the cumbrance that he had to
study out a better to pass it.   The man even sweat with the
labour, so that he was fain in the while now and then to
wipe his face.   Howbeit in conclusion, when it came to his
course, we that had spoken before him, had so taken all up
among us before, that we had not left him one wise word to
speak after.

Antony.—Alas ! good man, among so many of you, some .
good fellow should have lent him one.

Vincent.—It needed not, as hap was, Uncle, for he found
out such a shift, that in his flattering he passed us all the
many.

Antony.—Why, what said he, Cousin ?

Vincent.—By our Lady ! Uncle, not one word. . . . For
when he saw that he could find no word of praise that would
pass all that had been spoken before already, the wily fox
would speak never a word, but as he were ravished unto
heavenward with the wonder of the wisdom and eloquence
that my lord's grace had uttered in that oration, he fetched
a long sigh with an oh ! from the bottom of his breast, and
held up both his hands, and lifted up his head, and cast
up his eyes into the welkin and wept.

Antony.—Surely, Cousin, as Terence saith, such folks make
men of fools even stark mad, and much cause have their
lords to be right angry with them.

Vincent.—God hath indeed, and is, I ween : but as for
their lords, Uncle, if they would after wax angry with them
therefor, they should in my mind do them very great wrong,
when it is one of the things that they specially keep them

for. For those that are of such vainglorious mind (be they lords or be they meaner men) can be much better content to have their contents commended, then amended; and require their servants and their friend never so specially to tell them the very truth, yet shall he better please them if he speak them fair, than if he tell them truth. And in good faith, Uncle, the self-same prelate that I told you my tale of, I dare be bold to swear it (I know it so surely), had on a time made of his own drawing a certain treaty, that should serve for a league between that country and a great prince. In which treaty, himself thought that he had devised his articles so wisely, and indited them so well, that all the world would allow them. Whereupon longing sore to be praised, he called unto him a friend of his, a man well learned, and of good worship, and very well expert in those matters, as he that had been divers times ambassador for that country, and had made many such treaties himself. When he took him the treaty, and that he had read it, he asked him how he liked it, and said: " But I pray you heartily tell me the very truth ". And that he spake so heartily, that the other had weened he would fain have heard the truth, and in trust thereof he told him a fault therein. At the hearing whereof, he swore in great anger: " By the mass! thou art a very fool ". The other afterward told me, that he would never tell him truth again.

Antony.—Without question, Cousin, I cannot greatly blame him: and thus themself make every man mock them, flatter them, and deceive them : those, I say, that are of such vainglorious mind. For if they be content to hear the truth, let them then make much of those that tell them the truth, and withdraw their ear from them that falsely flatter them, and they shall be more truly served than with twenty requests, praying men to tell them true. King Ladislaus, our Lord assoil his soul, used much this manner among his servants. When any of them praised any deed of his, or any condition in him, if he perceived that they said but the truth, he would let it pass by uncontrolled. But when he saw that they set a gloss upon it for his praise of their own making beside, then would he shortly say unto them : " I pray thee, good fellow, when thou sayest grace at my board, never bring in *Gloria Patri* without a *sicut erat ;* that is to wit, even as it was, and none other- wise : and lift me not up with no lies, for I love it not ". If men would use this way with them, that this noble king used, it would minish much of their false flattery.

I can well allow, that men should commend (keeping them within the bounds of truth) such things as they see praiseworthy in other men, to give them the greater courage to the increase thereof. For men keep still in that point one condition of children, that praise must prick them forth ; but better it were to do well, and look for none. Howbeit, they that cannot find in their heart to commend another man's good deed, show themself either envious, or else of nature very cold and dull. But out of question, he that putteth his pleasure in the praise of the people hath but a fond phantasy. For if his finger do but ache of an hot blain, a great many men's mouths blowing out his praise will scantly do him among them all half so much ease as to have one little boy to blow upon his finger.[1]

[1] *Dialogue of Comfort*, Works, 1221.

PART THE FIFTH.

COLLOQUIAL AND QUAINT PHRASES.

COLLOQUIAL AND QUAINT PHRASES.

A faint faith is better than a strong heresy (423. D).

If God sit where He sat (570. F).

The old saw: Out of sight, out of mind (334. B).

It were as soon done to weave a new web of cloth as to sow up every hole in a net (224. A). [1]

The devil is ready to put out men's eyes that are content willingly to wax blind (341. F).

Each man knoweth well where his own shoe wringeth him.

It is in almost every country become a common proverb, that shame is as it is taken (1253. B).

When the wine were in and the wit out (243. B).

But yet, as women say: Somewhat it was always that the cat winked when her eye was out (241. A).

I admit the case as possible, but yet as such a case, as, I trust in God, this good man shall see the sky fall first and catch larks ere it happen (1022. B).

[1] Said of the tediousness of correcting a book full of errors.

I have espied this good man is a man of sadness and no great gamener.[1] For, if he were, he would never be angry for an angry word spoken by a man that is on the losing side. It is an old courtesy at the cards, perdie! to let the loser have his words (1018. F).[2]

Men use, if they have an evil turn, to write it in marble, and whoso doth us a good turn, we write it in dust (57. E).

He cannot see the wood for the trees (741. H).

If women might be suffered to begin once in the congregation to fall in disputing, those aspen. leaves of theirs would never leave wagging (769. B).[3]

A figure of rhetoric that men call sauce malapert (305. E).

Finding of a knot in a rush (778. G).

Sin it were to belie the devil (57. C).

A Jack of Paris, an evil pie twice baken (675. E).

To seek out one line in all St. Austin's works were to go look a needle in a meadow (837. H).

Men speak of some that bear two faces in **one hood** (271. G).

[1] Gamester.
[2] *Marg.* "But I can give the loser leave to chide." (Second Part of *Henry VI.*, act iii. scene 1.)
[3] The words are put in the mouth of Friar Barns.

We make the fashion of Christendom to seem all turned quite up so down (110. D).   Pervert and turn up so down the right order (242. E).[1]

Not worth a fig (241. G).   Not worth a straw (989. G, 464. C).   Not worth a rush (464. H).   Not worth a button (355. D).   On the other side set I not five straws (963. F).   Worth an aiglet of a good blue point (675. H). Cannot avail a fly (1143. B).

If the wager were but a butterfly I would never award him one wing (216. D).   I would not give the paring of a pear for his prayer, putting away the true faith therefrom as he doth (844. A).

Mad as a March hare ; Dead as a door nail ; Frushed to fitters [2] (374. T).   Drives me to the hard wall (596. B). They harp upon the right string (244. B).   Ever upon that string he harpeth (302. B).   Many wits rotten before ripe (841. F).   They can perceive chalk from cheese well enough (241. H).   The bones of buttered beer [3] (423. C).   Grass widows [4] (230. G).   A fair tale of a tub (371. H, 576. B). They tell us that all things is in Scripture as plain as a pack-staff (814. E).   Blasphemous and Bedlam-ripe (1036. H). Played bo-peep (841. G).   No more like than an apple to an oyster (724. C).   Less like than Paul's steeple to a dagger-sheath (595 H).   To make a lip [5] (294. F).

---

[1] So always, not up-side-down.
[2] *i.e.*, crushed to small fragments.—*Halliwell.*
[3] Beer boiled with lump sugar, butter and spice.
[4] An unmarried woman who has had a child.—*Halliwell.*
[5] To dissent from a proposition.

This is well devised and herein he playeth the good cow and giveth us a good gallon of milk (962. C).   Whoso shall read his worshipful writing shall perceive therein flourishing without fruit, subtilty without substance, rhetoric without reason, bold babbling without learning and wiliness without wit (291. F).[1]   Tindale's bibble-babble (641. E).

And thus, with this godly quip against me, for his *cum patre qui*, the good godly man maketh an end of his holy sermon and gaspeth a little and galpeth, and getteth him down from the pulpit (709. E).

Surely this anchor lieth too far aloof from this ship and hath never a cable to fasten her to it ; for never heard I yet two things so loosely knit together (759. C).

Except this young man (Frith) in these words of St. Austin see farther with his young sight than I can with mine old eyes and my spectacles, I marvel much that ever he would bring them in (838. B).

In which books Tindale showed himself so puffed up with the poison of pride, malice and envy, that it is more than marvel that the skin can hold together (283. B).

We see that this man fareth as one that walked bare-foot upon a field full of thorns, that wotteth not where to tread (535. C).   He scuddeth in and out like a hare that had twenty brace of greyhounds after her (721. E).

---

[1] Of Fish's *Supplication of Beggars.*

Yet in turning the one cheek from me he turneth the other very fair to me, so that he will have a clap on the one cheek or the other, make what shift he can (481. F).

———

Men might peradventure lay a block or twain in his way that would break his shins ere he leapt over it (539. C).

———

He will bring forth for the plain proof his old three worshipful witnesses, which stand yet all unsworn, that is to wit : Some-say, and They-say, and Folk-say (963. C).

———

He spinneth that fine lie with flax, fetching it out of his own body, as the spider spinneth her cobweb (940. C).

———

If this exposition of his mind may serve to quit him now (which I am content it do), it is all I promise you that it may do ; for it will never serve him to recover damages. For he can never blame no man that perceived not that before that is scarce credible now (945. D).

———

He speaketh much of mine unwritten dreams and vanities.[1] But here have we a written dream of his, and therein this foolish boast also, so full of vainglorious vanity, that if I had dreamed it in a fit of fever, I would (I ween) have been ashamed to have told my dream to my wife when I woke (1123. G).

———

Yet would the devil (I ween) disdain to have his supper dressed of such a rude ruffian, such a scald Colin cook (1136. F).

---

[1] Thus Tindale called " unwritten tratitions ".

In their only railing. standeth all their revel ; with only railing is their roast meat basted, and all their pot seasoned, and all their pie-meat spiced, and all their manchets, and all their wafers, and all their hippocras made (866. G).

————

If religious Lutherans may proceed and prosper, that cast off their habits and walk out and wed nuns and preach against purgatory, and make mocks of the mass, many men shall care little for obits within a while, and set no more by a trental than a ruffian at Rome setteth by a trent-une (880. D).

————

Tindale is as loth, good tender pernell, to take a little penance of the priest, as the lady was to come any more to disciplining,[1] that wept even for tender heart two days after when she talked of it, that the priest had on Good Friday with the disciplining rod beaten her hard upon her lily-white hands (893. F).

————

An Almain of mine acquaintance, when I blamed him lately for not fasting upon a certain day, answered me : " Fare to souid te laye men fasten ? let te prester fasten " ; etc. (895. H).

————

The Pacifier saith that the judge may be partial and " the witness may be a wolf showing himself apparelled in the apparel of a lamb " ; which appearing in apparel, poor men that cannot apparel their speech with the apparel of rhetoric, use commonly to call " a wolf in a lamb's skin " ! (910. F).

[1] Dyspelyng.

It is now a world to see with what a courage and boldness he boasteth and rejoiceth, and what a joy he maketh,
as he were even made a king by the finding of a bean in a
Christmas cake (776. H).[1]

He is loth to say that these be heretics, but he sayeth :
" These be they that men call heretics ". Wherein he
speaketh much like as if he would point with his finger to a
flock of fat wethers, and say : " These be such beasts as
men call sheep " (330. B).

In the mean season they be content to play the wily foxes
and worry simple souls and poor lambs as they may catch
them straggling from the fold, or rather like a false shep-
herd's-dog, that would but bark in sight and seem to fetch
in the sheep, and yet kill a lamb in a corner (271. G).

Tindale's defence of his translating *presbyteros* into elders
is as feeble to stick to as is an old rotten elder stick (426.
H).

Having a little wanton money, which him thought[2]
burned out the bottom of his purse, in the first year of his
wedding took his wife with him and went over sea, for none
other errand but to see Flanders and France and ride out
one summer in those countries (195. B).

[1] Formerly children played at king and queen on the Epiphany.
A bean was hidden in a cake, which was cut in slices and distributed.
The owner of the bean was the king. The game was still played in
my youth.—EDITOR.

[2] It seemed to him.

A tale that fleeth through many mouths catcheth many feathers, which when they be pulled away again leave him as pilled as a coot (238. B).

. He laugheth but from the lips forward, and grinneth as a dog doth when one porreth him in the teeth with a stick (432. F).

After his own sweet will (367. F). Alas! for the dear mercy of God (837. F). God-a-mercy for right naught (757. D). It is *a world to see* the blindness that the devil hath driven into him (1090. F, 1099. F). Ugly gargoyle faces (354. G). A stretch-hemp[1] (715. A).

Be not so led with a few painted holy words, as it were with the beholding of a peacock's tail, but that ye regard therewith his foul feet also (359. A).

As wise as one that, lest his rotten house should fall, would go about to take down the roof and pull up the groundsill to undershore the sides with the same (473. E).

Till we lie in our death-bed, where we shall have so many things to do at once, and everything so unready, *that every finger shall be a thumb*, and we shall fumble it all up in haste so unhandsomely that we may hap to leave more than half undone (1299. C).

We shall for this matter trouble you no longer, but every man may take holy water and go home to dinner, for service is all done here to-day (942. E).

[1] A villain likely to be hung.

A fond old man is often as full of words as a woman.   It is, you wot well, as some of the poets paint us, all the lust of an old fool's life, to sit well and warm, with a cup and roasted crab, and drivel and drink and talk (1169. F).

So help me God and none otherwise, but as I verily think that many a man buyeth hell with so much pain, that he might have heaven with less than the one half (1203. E).

Though that, to the repressing of the bold courage of blind youth, there is a very true proverb, that as soon cometh a young sheep's skin to the market as an old ; yet this difference there is at the least between them, that as the young man may hap sometime to die soon, so the old man can never live long (1172. E).

I wist once a great officer of the king's say (and in good faith I ween he said but as he thought) that twenty men, standing barehead before him, kept not his head half so warm as to keep on his own cap.   Nor he never took so much ease with their being barehead before him, as he caught once grief with a cough that came upon him by standing barehead long before the king (1224. G).

A like learned priest that throughout all the gospels scraped out *diabolus* and wrote *Jesus Christus*, because he thought the devil's name was not meet to stand in so good a place (421. B).

I never saw fool yet that thought himself other than wise. For as it is one spark of soberness left in a drunken head, when he perceiveth himself drunk and getteth him fair to bed, so if a fool perceive himself a fool, that point is no folly, but a little spark of wit (1251. B).

If Adam had abiden in paradise many years more than he did, and had afterwards before his translation, upon the suggestion of the *old serpent the devil, and of the young serpent the woman,* eaten of the fruit as he did, he had in any time of his life had the selfsame fall (1289. D).

Covetice (covetousness) is a very prisoner, for he cannot get away. Pride will away with shame, envy with his enemy's misery, wrath with fair entreating, sloth with hunger and pain, lechery with sickness, gluttony with the belly too full, but covetice can nothing get away. For the more full, the more greedy; and the older the more niggard; and the richer the more needy (1297. G).

He that biddeth other folk do well, and giveth evil example with the contrary deed himself, fareth even like a foolish weaver, that would weave a part with his one hand and unweave a part with his other (1319. E).

Commonly, as Juvenal saith, great men's houses be well stored with saucy malapert merchants,[1] and men learn by their own experience, that, in every country, noblemen's servants be statelier and much more extreme than are their lords themselves (1390. H).

[1] *i.e.,* fellows.

CLERICAL TONSURE.

Tindale.—Because they be all shaven, so be they all shameless to affirm that they be the right church, etc.

More.—When he hath, about the proof of this point, bestowed already his whole chapter afore, wherein he came forward, perdie ! with his five eggs, and after a great face made of a great feast, supped them all up himself without any salt—for all his guests that he bade to supper might smell them so rotten that they supped off the savour—now to come forth again with the same tale, and set us to the same table at supper again, with neither bread nor drink, flesh, fish nor fruit ! This man well declareth as that though he be not shaven, but hath the hair of his unshaven crown grown out at great length, in despite of priesthood, and like an Iceland cur[1] let hang over his eyes, yet hath the man as much shame in his face as a shotten[2] herring hath shrimps in her tail (626).

FAST.

St. John lived in desert and fasted and fared hard, and lay hard, and watched and prayed.   These folk live in great towns, and fare well and fast not, no not so much as the three golden Fridays—that is to wit, the Friday next after Palm Sunday, and the Friday next afore Easter day, and Good Friday—but will eat flesh upon all three, and utterly love no Lenten fast, nor lightly no fast else, saving break-fast, and eat-fast and drink-fast and sleep-fast and lusk-fast in their lechery, and then come forth and rail fast. This was not the manner of rebuking that St. John used.   And

[1] Skye terrier.   [2] Gutted and dried.

therefore Tindale saith untrue, when he saith they rebuke after the same manner that St John did the Jews (651. G).

MORE'S BANTER.

Tindale's héresy reckoneth every woman a priest, and as able to say mass as was ever St. Peter. And in good faith, as for such masses as he would have said, without the canon, without the secrets, without oblation, without sacrifice, without the Body or Blood of Christ, with bare signs and tokens instead of the B. Sacrament, I ween a woman were indeed a more meet priest than St. Peter.

And albeit that neither woman may be priest, nor any man is priest or bath power to say mass, but if he be by the sacrament of holy orders taken and consecrated into that offiee ; yet since the time that Tindale hath begun his heresies and sent his erroneous books about, calling every Christian woman a priest, there is not now in some places of England the simplest woman in the parish, but that she doth, and that not in corners secretly, but look on who will, in open face of the world, in her own parish church, I say not bear but *say* her own self, and (lest you should look for some riddle) openly revested at the high altar, she *saith* (I say) herself and singeth too (if it be true that I hear reported) as many masses in one week, as Tindale himself either saith or heareth in two whole years together.[1]

More does not mean that any woman put on the vestments and said or sung mass, but that they did it as often as Tindale, *i.e.*, never. He liked sometimes thus to mystify others.

ANOTHER EXAMPLE.

Tindale.—" Now, theiefore, when they ask us how we

[1] *Conf. of Tindale*, Works, 622.

know that it is the Scripture of God, ask them who taught
the eagles to spy out their prey.   Even so the children of
God spy out their Father, and Christ's elect spy out their
Lord, and trace out the paths of His feet."

More.—He proveth his point by the ensample of a very
goodly bird and king of all fowls, the pleasant splayed eagle.
For since that such a bird can spy his prey untaught, which he
could never do but by the secret instinct of his excellent nature,
so far exceeding all other, it must needs follow, perdie! that
Tindale and Luther in likewise, and Huskin,[1] and Zuinglius
and such other excellent heretics, being in God's favour as far
above all the Catholic Church as an eagle, the rich royal king
of all birds, is above a poor penny chicken, must needs, without any learning of any man, be taught to know the true
Scripture, being their prey to spoil and kill and devour it
as they list, even by the especial inspiration of God.

But now ye see well, good readers, by this reason, that
St. Austin, in respect of these noble eagles that spy their
prey without the means of the Church, was but a silly poor
chicken.   For he confesseth plainly, against such high eagle
heretics, that himself had not known nor believed the Gospel
but by the Catholic Church.   Howbeit, it is no great marvel,
since God is not so familiar with such simple chickens, as
w'th His gay, glorious eagles.   But one thing is there that
I cannot cease to marvel of, since God inspireth Tindale and
such other eagles, and thereby maketh them spy their prey
themselves, how could it happen that the goodly golden old
eagle, Martin Luther himself, in whose goodly golden nest
this young eagle-bird was hatched, lacked that inspiration?
For he alloweth St. Austin's saying, and denieth not but

[1] Œcolampadius.

that himself spied and perceived this prey of the true Scripture of God by being showed it by the Catholic Church.

Howbeit I wis when our young eagle Tindale learned to
spy this prey first, he was not yet full-feathered, but scantily
come out of the shell, nor so high flickered in the air above
all our heads to learn it of his father, the old eagle-heretic,
but was content to come down here and walk on the ground
among other poor fowls, the poor children of his mother, of
whom, when he hath all said, he learned to know this prey.[1]

An Apt Simile.

These heretics always, for the proof of their heresies, seek
out the hardest places that can be found in Scripture, and
all the plain, open words, in which can be no doubt or question, they come and expound by those places that be dark,
obscure, and hard to understand; much like a blind guide,
that would, when men were walking in a dark night, put
out the candle and show them the way with the lanthorn.[2]

Another.

These heretics be almost as many sects as men, and never
one agreeth with other. So that if the world were to learn
the right way of them, that matter were much like as if a man
walking in a wilderness, that fain would find the right way towards the town that he intended, should meet with a many [i.e.,
a company] of lewd, mocking knaves, which, when the poor
man had prayed them to tell him the way, would get them into
a roundel, turning them back to back, and then speak all at
once, and each of them tell him "this way!" each of them
pointing forth with his hand the way that his face standeth.[3]

[1] *Conf. of Tindale*, Works, 684.
[2] *Ibid.*, Works, 541. E.
[3] *Ibid.*, Works, 707.

INDEX.

15*

INDEX.

(235)

Sermons, sleeping at, 17.

    ,,   way of concluding, 222.

Shame, endured for God, 81.

Sin, mortal and venial, 33.

Slander of classes, 62.

Sorrow for sin, 47, 121.

Spirituality, false, 128.

Stage plays, 178.

Strangeness, 160.

Superstition, 174.

Tales, use of, 183.

        Sleeping at sermon, 17.

        Cure for toothache, 36 ; a charm, 174.

        Man sea-sick, 42.

        A sick physician, 50.

        Last words of a blasphemer, 46.

        A cut-purse, 59.

        Trust in the devil, 64.

        Limited faith, 187.

        Blind impostor and Duke Humphrey, 161.

        Travellers' lies, 158.

        Was our Lady a Jewess ? 163.

        Cure of possessed girl, 163.

        Image at Barking, 166.

        Cliff the Fool, 183.

        Paterson the Fool, 194.

        Davy the Dutchman, 193.

        Grime, the mustard maker, 184.

        Origen, 191.

        Luther's marriage, 187.

        Gallant and friar, 185.

        Fears of the night, 200.

        A sophister, 191.

        A riddle, 191.

        Provoking wife, 202.

        Talkative wife, 210.

        Strange surety, 185.

        Strange temptation, 199.

        Carver's wife, 190.

        Maid and tiler, 186.

WORKS BY THE REV. T. E. BRIDGETT.

LIFE OF BLESSED THOMAS MORE.
Price 7s. 6d.

LIFE OF BLESSED JOHN FISHER.
Second Edition.   With Appendix.
Price 7s. 6d.

HISTORY OF THE HOLY EUCHARIST IN GREAT BRITAIN.
2 vols.   Price 18s.

OUR LADY'S DOWRY:
How England Won that Title.   Third Edition.   Illustrated.
Price 5s.

TRUE STORY OF THE CATHOLIC HIERARCHY DEPOSED BY QUEEN ELIZABETH,
with fuller Memoirs of its Last Two Survivors.   Price 7s. 6d.

BLUNDERS AND FORGERIES.
Price 6s.

THE DISCIPLINE OF DRINK:
An Essay on the Use, Abuse, and *Disuse* of Alcoholic *Drinks*, especially in the British Isles before the Sixteenth Century.
Price 3s. 6d.

THE RITUAL OF THE NEW TESTAMENT:
An Essay on the Principles and Origin of Catholic Ritual.
Third Edition.   Price 5s.

RETREAT FOR MEN.
Second Edition.   Price 1s.

Edited by the Rev. T. E. Bridgett.
THE SUPPLIANT OF THE HOLY GHOST.
From a Seventeenth Century MS.
Price 1s. 6d.

SOULS DEPARTED:
Being a *Defence* and *Declaration* of the Catholic Church's *Doctrine* touching Purgatory and Prayers for the *Dead*.
By CARDINAL ALLEN.   With Portrait.   Price 6s.

BURNS & OATES, LTD., LONDON AND NEW YORK.

BURNS & OATES' PUBLICATIONS

A SELECTION

Threepence in the Shilling off all Books, except NET Books, for Cash with order

A Complete Catalogue including Foreign Books Free on Application

28 ORCHARD STREET
. LONDON
W

Telegrams
Burns Oates London

Telephone
2706 Mayfair

THE WORKS OF
FRANCIS THOMPSON

POEMS. 5s. net.

"Crashaw born again, but born greater."—*Daily Chronicle.*

SISTER SONGS. 5s. net.

" A book that Shelley would have adored."—*William Archer.*

NEW POEMS. 6s. net.

" Poems that are matchless for their beauty of idea and expression."
Black and White.

SELECTED POEMS. 5s. net.

With a Biographical Note by Wilfrid Meynell, and a Portrait of the Poet

" Here is the essence of the most remarkable of recent English
Poets."—*Times.*

PUBLISHED SEPARATELY.

THE HOUND OF HEAVEN. 1s. net.

" It is the return of the nineteenth century to Thomas à Kempis."

HIS PROSE IS HEROIC.—Spectator.

HEALTH AND HOLINESS. 2s. net.

A Study of the Relations between Brother Ass, the Body, and his
Rider, the Soul.   With a Preface by the Rev. George Tyrrell.

SHELLEY. 2s. 6d. net.

Large paper edition, 5s. net.

Just out.

An Essay.   With an Appreciation by the Rt. Hon. George
Wyndham, M.P.

" It is the most important contribution to pure Letters written in
English during the last twenty years."—*Mr. Wyndham.*

MEDITATIONS AND DEVOTIONS.

À KEMPIS, THOMAS.

Of the Imitation of Christ. *The Seraphic Edition.* Being an entirely new translation from the Latin by FATHER THADDEUS, O.F.M. Cloth, 6/- net ; leather, 7/6 net. *Popular Edition*, 6d. and 1/-. *Superfine Pocket Edition*, from 1/6 to 10/-. *Presentation Edition*, from 3/6 to 15/-.

AT THE FEET OF JESUS. By MADAME CECILIA. 2/6.

DEVOTIONAL LIBRARY FOR CATHOLIC HOUSEHOLDS. Containing : New Testament, Book of Psalms, Imitation of Christ, Devout Life, Spiritual Combat. Cloth, **red** edges, with cloth case to match. 5/- net (postage 4d.).

DOLOROUS PASSION OF OUR LORD JESUS CHRIST. From the Meditations of ANNE CATHERINE EMMERICH. 3/6.

FATHER DIGNAM'S RETREAT. 6/- net (postage 4d.).

FATHER FABER.

All for Jesus : or, The Easy Ways of Divine Love. 5/-.

Bethlehem. 7/-.

Growth in Holiness : or, The Progress of the Spiritual Life. 6/-.

Notes on Doctrinal and Spiritual Subjects. Two Vols. 10/-.

Spiritual Conferences. 6/-.

The Creator and the Creature : or, The Wonders of Divine Love. 6/-.

The Precious Blood : or, The Price of our Salvation. 5/-.

FEASTS OF MOTHER CHURCH. With Hints and Help for the Holier Keeping of them. By MOTHER M SALOME. Illustrated. 3/6.

FRANCIS DE SALES, ST.

Introduction to the Devout Life. Cloth, red edges 1/6. Calf, red edges, 5s. Morocco, gilt edges, 5/6.

The Mystical Explanation of the Canticle o Canticles. Also St. Jane Frances de Chantal' Depositions in the Cause of the Beatification an Canonization of St. Francis de Sales. 6/-.

Spiritual Conferences of St. Francis de Sales Translated, with Additions and Notes, under th supervision of ABBOT GASQUET, O.S.B., and the lat CANON MACKEY, O.S.B. 6/-.

Letters to Persons in the World. 6/-.

The Treatise on the Love of God. 6/-.

GERTRUDE AND MECHTILDE, THE PRAYERS OF SS Cloth, 1/-. Leather, 2/- and 4/6.

GERTRUDE, THE EXERCISES OF ST. Cloth, 1/6 Leather, 2/- and 4/6.

GROWTH IN THE KNOWLEDGE OF OUR LORD. Medita tions for every Day of the Year. Adapted from th Original of the Abbé de Brandt. By MOTHER MAR FIDELIS. In Three Volumes. 21/-. net (postage 7d.).

HOLY WISDOM (*Sancta Sophia*). Directions for the Praye of Contemplation, &c. By VEN. FATHER F. AUGUSTI BAKER, O. S. B. Edited by ABBOT SWEENEY, D. Quarter leather, 5/-. *Cheaper*, 3/6.

I AM THE WAY. By FATHER NEPVEU, S.J. With Preface by the Archbishop of Westminster. 2/6 n (postage 3d.).

IMITATION OF THE SACRED HEART OF JESUS. I Four Books. By Rev. FATHER ARNOLD, S.J. Cloth, 4/ Cloth, gilt, red edges, 5/-. Leather, 8/6.

LENTEN READINGS. From the Writings of the Fathers and Doctors of the Church as found in the Roman Breviary. Done into English by JOHN PATRICK, Marquess of Bute, and arranged by FATHER JOHN MARY, O.S.F.C. 2/6.

MEDITATIONS ON THE SACRED HEART. By the Rev. JOSEPH EGGER, S.J. Cloth, gilt. 2/6.

PATERNOSTER, ST. TERESA'S. A Treatise or Prayer. By Very Rev. JOSEPH FRASSINETTI. 4/-.

RETREAT, A. By BISHOP HEDLEY, O.S.B. For the use of the Clergy, Religious and others. 6/-.

RETREAT MANUAL, THE. A Handbook for the Annual Retreat and Monthly Recollection. By MADAME CECILIA. Preface by the Rev. Sidney Smith, S.J. 2/-.

SCUPOLI'S SPIRITUAL COMBAT. With the Supplement and the Treatise on Inward Peace. Size, 5 by 3¼ inches. Cloth, 6d. net (postage 2d.). Cloth, gilt, red edges, 1/-. Lambskin, 2/6. Calf and Morocco, 4/6.

SPIRIT OF THE CURE D'ARS, THE. From the French of M. l'Abbé MONNIN. Edited by Rev. JOHN E. BOWDEN, of the Oratory. With Portrait. 2/-.

SPIRITUAL ASCENT, THE. A Devotional Treatise by GERARD OF ZUTPHEN. 2/6 net (postage 3d.).

SPIRITUAL RETREAT. By Rev. REGINALD BUCKLER, O.P. 3/6 net (postage 4d.).

STATIONS OF THE CROSS. By HERBERT THURSTON, S.J. 3/6 net (postage 4d.).

TOWARDS ETERNITY. By the ABBÉ POULIN. Translated by M. T. TORROMÉ. 5/-.

ULLATHORNE, ARCHBISHOP.

Christian Patience, the Strength and Discipline of the Soul. 7/-.

The Endowments of Man considered in their Relations with his Final End. 7/-.

The Groundwork of the Christian Virtues. 7/-.

The Little Book of Humility and Patience. Bein a Selection from Archbishop Ullathorne's two volumes With a Portrait. 2/- net.

WATERS THAT GO SOFTLY: or, Thoughts for time o Retreat. By Fr. RICKABY, S.J. 2/6

WISEMAN, CARDINAL.

A Month's Meditations. Leather back. 4/-.

Meditations on the Sacred Passion of Our Lord. 4/-

Meditations on the Incarnation and Life of Ou Lord. 4/-.

ON THE BLESSED SACRAMENT AND
HOLY COMMUNION.

AT HOME NEAR THE ALTAR. By Rev. MATTHEW RUSSELL S. J. Cloth, gilt. 1/- net (postage 1½d.).

BANQUET OF THE ANGELS, THE. Preparation an Thanksgiving for Holy Communion. By ARCHBISHO PORTER, S.J. Blue Cloth, gilt, 2/-. Leather bindings suitable for First Communion memorials, 6/6 net an 8/6 net.

CLOSE TO THE ALTAR RAILS. By the Rev. MATTHEV RUSSELL, S.J. Cloth, gilt. 1/- net (postage 1½d.).

DIVINE CONSOLER, THE. Little Visits to the Most Hol Sacrament. By J. M. ANGÉLI, of the Lazarist Fathers Translated by GENEVIÈVE IRONS. 2/6.

FABER, FATHER.

The Blessed Sacrament: or, the Works and Way of God. 7/6.

HISTORY OF THE HOLY EUCHARIST IN GREAT BRITAIN By T. E. BRIDGETT, C.SS.R. Edited with Notes b FATHER H. THURSTON, S.J. Folio. Illustrated. On Guinea net.

HOLY SACRIFICE AND ITS CEREMONIES, THE. B FATHER NIEUWBARN, O.P. This book has been selling by thousands in Dutch. Now issued in English, wit Illustrations, 2/-.

FIRST COMMUNION. A Book of Preparation for First Communion. By MOTHER MARY LOYOLA. Edited by FATHER THURSTON, S.J. Illustrated. 3/6.

FIRST COMMUNION, QUESTIONS ON. By MOTHER M. LOYOLA. 1/-.

LEGENDS OF THE BLESSED SACRAMENT : Gathered from the History of the Church and the Lives of the Saints. By EMILY MARY SHAPCOTE. With numerous Illustrations. Cloth, gilt. 6/-.

MANNING, CARDINAL.

The Blessed Sacrament the Centre of Immutable Truth. Cloth, gilt. 1/-.

MOMENTS BEFORE THE TABERNACLE. By Rev. MATTHEW RUSSELL, S.J. 1/- net (postage 1d.).

REFLECTIONS AND PRAYERS FOR HOLY COMMUNION. With Preface by Cardinal Manning. In Two Volumes, each complete in itself. 4/6 each. Cloth, red edges, 5/- each. Leather, 9/- and 10/- each.

SACRIFICE OF THE MASS, THE. An Explanation of its Doctrine, Rubrics, and Prayers. By Rev. M. GAVIN, S.J. 2/-.

TREASURE OF THE CHURCH, THE. By CANON J. B. BAGSHAWE, D.D. 3/6.

VISITS TO THE MOST HOLY SACRAMENT AND THE BLESSED VIRGIN MARY. By ST. ALPHONSUS LIGUORI. Edited by BISHOP COFFIN, C.SS.R. Cloth, 1/-. Leather, 2/6 and 4/6.

WELCOME ! Holy Communion, Before and After. By MOTHER MARY LOYOLA. Edited by FATHER THURSTON, S.J. With Frontispiece of Holman Hunt's "Light of the World." 3/6 net. Prayer-book size, handsomely bound, red under gilt edges, 5/- net (postage 4d.).

ON THE BLESSED VIRGIN.

BLESSED VIRGIN IN THE FATHERS OF THE FIRST SIX CENTURIES, THE. By Rev. THOMAS LIVIUS, M.A., C.SS.R. 12/-.

BLESSED VIRGIN IN THE NINETEENTH CENTURY, THE. Apparitions, Revelations, Graces. By BERNARD ST. JOHN. With Introduction by Rev. E. Thiriet, O.M.I. Illustrated. 6/-.

FABER, FATHER.
The Foot of the Cross : or, The Sorrows of Mary. 6/-.
Father Faber's May Book. Cloth, gilt edges. 2/-.

GLORIES OF MARY, THE. By ST. ALPHONSUS LIGUORI. Edited by BISHOP COFFIN, C.SS.R. 3/6.

MADONNA, THE. A Pictorial Record of the Life and Death of the Mother of our Lord Jesus Christ by the Painters and Sculptors of Christendom in more than Five Hundred of their Works. The Text translated from the Italian of ADOLFO VENTURI, with an Introduction by ALICE MEYNELL. Bound in Buckram. £1 11s. 6d.

MARY IMMACULATE. From the Writings of the Fathers and Doctors of the Church as found in the Roman Breviary. Done into English by JOHN PATRICK, Marquess of Bute, and compiled by FATHER JOHN MARY, Capuchin Friar Minor. Cloth, 1/- net (postage 2d.). Leather, 2/6 net (postage 2d.)

MARY IN THE EPISTLES. By Rev. T. LIVIUS, M.A., C.SS.R. 5/-.

MARY IN THE GOSPELS. Lectures on the History of Our Blessed Lady, as recorded by the Evangelists. By Very Rev. J. SPENCER NORTHCOTE. 3/6.

MONTH OF MARY. By Very Rev. FATHER BECKX, S.J. 3/-.

MONTH OF MARY. By ST. ALPHONSUS LIGUORI. 1/6.

OUR LADY'S MANUAL : or, Devotions to the Sacred Heart of Mary. Cloth, 2/-. Best Cloth, red edges, 2/6. Calf or Morocco, 5/6 each.

OUR LADY OF PERPETUAL SUCCOUR. A Manual of Devotion for every day of the Month. Translated from the French by Rev. T. LIVIUS, C.SS.R. Cloth, 1/- net. Leather, 2/- net, 2/6 net, and 4/6 net (postage 2d.).

OUR LADY OF PERPETUAL SUCCOUR, MANUAL OF. From the Writings of St. Alphonsus Liguori. By a Redemptorist Father. 1/- and 2/- net. With hymns, 1/6 and 3/- net (postage 3d.).

SINLESS MARY AND SINFUL MARY. I.—Mary's Social Mission as the Second Eve. II.—The Woman that was a Sinner. By FATHER BERNARD VAUGHAN, S.J. With Two Illustrations. Leather, 3/6 net. Cloth, 2/- net. Stiff wrapper, 1/- net (postage 2d.).

TREATISE ON THE TRUE DEVOTION TO THE BLESSED VIRGIN MARY. By Blessed GRIGNON DE MONTFORT. 2/-.

WORLD'S MADONNA, THE. By J. S. MULHOLLAND, B.L. 2/6 net.

THEOLOGICAL AND APOLOGETICAL.

CATHOLIC CONTROVERSY. A Reply to Dr. Littledale's "Plain Reasons." By Very Rev. H. I. D. RYDER, of the Oratory. 1/- net (postage 3d.).

CATHOLIC CONTROVERSY, THE. By ST. FRANCIS DE SALES. Edited by Very Rev. CANON MACKEY, O.S.B. 6/-.

CONTROVERSIAL CATECHISM. By the Rev. STEPHEN KEENAN. 2/-.

FAITH AND FOLLY. By MGR. JOHN S. VAUGHAN. 5/- net. (postage 4d.).

FORMATION OF CHRISTENDOM, THE. By T. W. ALLIES, K.C.S.G. *New and Revised Edition.* 5/- each volume.
Vol. I. The Christian Faith and the Individual.—Vol. II. The Christian Faith and Society.—Vol. III. The Christian Faith and Philosophy.—Vol. IV. As seen in Church and State.—Vol. V. The Throne of the Fisherman.

FREE WILL AND FOUR ENGLISH PHILOSOPHERS. A Study of Hobbes, Locke, Hume and Mill. By FATHER JOSEPH RICKABY, S.J. 3/6 net (postage 3d.).

MANNING, CARDINAL.

    Sin and its Consequences. 4/-.

    The Glories of the Sacred Heart. 4/-.

    The Four Great Evils of the Day. 2/6.

    The Fourfold Sovereignty of God. 2/6.

    The Holy Ghost the Sanctifier. Cloth, gilt. 2/-.

    The Independence of the Holy See. 2/6.

    The Temporal Mission of the Holy Ghost: or, Reaso and Revelation. Cr. 8vo. 5/-.

    The Workings of the Holy Spirit in the Church o England. 1/6.

    Why I Became a Catholic. (Religio Viatoris). 1/-.

NATURAL RELIGION. Being Vol. I. of Dr. HETTINGER' "Evidences of Christianity." Edited by Rev. H. S BOWDEN. With an Introduction on "Certainty." 7/6.

OF GOD AND HIS CREATURES. An Annotated translation with some Abridgments, of the *Summa Contra Gentile* of St. Thomas Aquinas. By Rev. JOSEPH RICKABY, S.J. Foolscap folio. One Guinea net (postage 9d.).

PETER, ST., BISHOP OF ROME : or, the Roman Epis copate of the Prince of the Apostles. By Rev. T LIVIUS, M.A., C.SS.R. 12/-.

RELIGION OF THE PLAIN MAN. By FATHER R. H BENSON, 2/6 net (postage 3d.).

REVEALED RELIGION. The Second Volume of Dr HETTINGER'S "Evidences of Christianity." Edited b Rev. H. S. BOWDEN. With an Introduction on th "Assent of Faith." 5/-.

SUPPLIANT OF THE HOLY GHOST : A Paraphrase of th "Veni Sancte Spiritus." By Rev. R. JOHNSON, o Louvain. Edited by Rev. T. E. BRIDGETT, C.SS.R. 1/6

SERMONS AND DISCOURSES.

BISHOP HEDLEY, O.S.B.

    Christian Inheritance, The. Set forth in Sermons. 6/-

    Light of Life, The. Set forth in Sermons. 6/-.

    Our Divine Saviour. 6/-.

MANNING, CARDINAL.
Sermons on Ecclesiastical Subjects. 6/-.

ERMON COMPOSITION. A Method for Students. By Rev. GEORGE S. HITCHCOCK, B.A., Lond., Minerva University, Rome. With a Preface by the Rev. Bernard Vaughan, S.J. 2/6 net.

ERMON DELIVERY. (*In the press.*) By the same Author. 2/6 net.

ERMONS FOR THE SUNDAYS AND FESTIVALS OF THE YEAR. By Rt. Rev. ABBOT SWEENEY, O.S.B 7/6.

BIBLES AND PRAYER BOOKS.

ATHOLIC'S DAILY COMPANION. 1/- to 5/-.

ATHOLIC'S VADE MECUM. 3/6 to 21/-.

AILY PRAYER BOOK, THE. Leather. 2/- net (postage 3d.).

LOWERS OF DEVOTION. *New Vest-pocket Edition.* With Ordinary of the Mass in large type. In leather bindings at 1/6, 2/6, 4/-, 5/-, and 6/.

ARDEN OF THE SOUL. In Five Editions. 6d. to 17/6.

OLDEN MANUAL, THE. The most complete Prayer Book. 6/- to 30/-.

OLY BIBLE. *Octavo Edition* (9 by 6 inches). Cloth, red edges, 5/-; and in a great variety of Leather Bindings, at 8/-, 10/-, 15/-, 18/-, 30/-, and 35/- each. *Pocket Edition* (size 5¼ by 3¼ inches): Embossed Cloth, red edges, 2/6; and in Leather Bindings at 4/6, 6/6 and 7/6.

EY OF HEAVEN. In Three Editions. 6d. net to 5/-.

MANUAL OF CATHOLIC PIETY. In Three Editions. 6d. net to 5/-.

ANUAL OF PRAYERS FOR CONGREGATIONAL USE. *New Pocket Edition* with Epistles and Gospels. (5 by 3¼ inches). 369 pages. Cloth, 6d. net (postage 2d.). Or with an Enlarged Appendix, Cloth, 1/-. Leather, 2/6, 5/-, and upwards.

ANUAL OF THE SACRED HEART. Cloth, 2/-. Cloth, red edges, with Frontispiece, 2/6. Leather, 4/6, 5/6, and 6/-.

ISSAL FOR THE LAITY. 6d. net to 5/-.

NEW TESTAMENT. *Large-Type Edition.* With annotations, references, and an historical and chronological index. Cr. 8vo (size 7½ by 5 inches). 500 pp. **Cloth,** 2/-; and in leather bindings at 4/6 and 8/6. *Pocket Edition*: Limp cloth, 6d. net (postage 2d.); Cloth, red edges, 1/-; Leather bindings, 1/6, 3/- and 4/6.

PATH TO HEAVEN. *New and Enlarged Edition.* (Over 1,000 pages). 2/- to 8/6.

ROMAN MISSAL. With all the New Offices, and the Propers for England, Ireland, Scotland, the Society of Jesus, and the Order of St. Benedict. Size 5⅞ by 3⅞ inches. 5/- to 30/-.

SPIRIT OF THE SACRED HEART. 3/6, 5/6, 8/6, and 12/6. 700 pages, printed in large clear type.

THE YOUNG CHILD'S MASS-BOOK. By the Hon. Mrs. KAVANAGH. *Popular Edition*, Cloth, 6d. *New and Revised Edition*, re-set in large type, and with 10 specially-designed coloured Illustrations. Cloth, gilt, gilt edges, 1/-. Lambskin, limp, gilt edges, 2/6.

ON THE PRIESTHOOD AND ON RELIGIOUS LIFE.

CATECHISM OF THE VOWS. By Rev. P. COTEL, S.J. 1/-.

INWARD GOSPEL, THE. Some familiar discourses addressed to Religious who follow the Rules of St. Ignatius. By W. D. STRAPPINI, S.J. 2/6 net (postage 3d.). *Just out.*

LETTERS TO PERSONS IN RELIGION. By ST. FRANCIS DE SALES. With Introduction by Bishop Hedley. 6/-.

MANNING, CARDINAL. The Eternal Priesthood. 3/6.

PARISH PRIEST'S PRACTICAL MANUAL, NEW. A Work useful also for other Ecclesiastics, especially for Confessors and for Preachers. By Very Rev. JOSEPH FRASSINETTI. Translated by ARCHDEACON HUTCH, D.D. 6/-.

PRACTICAL MEDITATIONS FOR EVERY DAY IN THE YEAR, on the Life of Our Lord Jesus Christ. Chiefly for the use of Religious. By a Father of the Society of Jesus. In Two Volumes. Cloth. 9/-.

RELIGIOUS LIFE AND THE VOWS, THE. A Treatise by MGR. CHARLES GAY, Bishop of Anthedon. 5/-.

SALVATORI'S PRACTICAL INSTRUCTIONS FOR NEW CONFESSORS. Edited by FATHER ANTHONY BALLERINI, S.J., and Translated by ARCHDEACON HUTCH, D.D. 18mo. Cloth, gilt. 4/-.

THE YOUNG PRIEST : Conferences on the Apostolic Life. By HERBERT CARDINAL VAUGHAN. Edited by MGR. CANON J. S. VAUGHAN. 5/- net (postage 4d.).

BIOGRAPHY AND HAGIOLOGY.

ACTON, LORD, AND HIS CIRCLE. Edited by ABBOT GASQUET. With an Engraved Portrait of Lord Acton. 15/- net.

ALLIES, THOMAS WILLIAM. A Biography. By his daughter, MARY ALLIES. With Two Portraits and other Illustrations. 3/6 net (postage 4d.).

ANSELM OF CANTERBURY, ST. By Right Rev. MGR. MOYES. 6d. net.

BRIEFE HISTORIE OF THE GLORIOUS MARTYRDOM OF XII PRIESTS, Edmund Campion and his Companions. By CARDINAL ALLEN. Edited by Rev. J. H. POLLEN, S.J. 4/- net.

BUTLER, REV. ALBAN.

— **Complete Lives of the Saints for Every Day in the Year.** Twelve Pocket Monthly Volumes and Index Volume, in neat cloth binding, gilt lettered, 1/6 each. Or the complete set of Thirteen Volumes, in handsome cloth case, 20/-.

CAMPION, EDMUND, LIFE OF. By RICHARD SIMPSON. 12/-

CATHERINE DE RICCI, ST. : HER LIFE, HER LETTERS, HER COMMUNITY. By F. M. CAPES. Introduced by a Treatise on the Mystical Life by Father Bertrand Wilberforce, O.P. With a Portrait of the Saint, a Facsimile Letter, and other Illustrations. 7/6 net.

CURE D'ARS, LIFE OF THE. From the French of ABBÉ MONNIN. Edited by CARDINAL MANNING. F'cap 8vo. Illustrated wrapper. 1/- net. Cloth, gilt. 2/6.

D'OSSEVILLE, LIFE OF MOTHER SAINTE MARIE HEN RIETTE LE FORESTIER, Foundress of the Society o the Faithful Virgin. With an Appreciation by th Archbishop of Westminster. 5/- net (postage 4d.).

LUMMIS, MADAME ROSE. By DELIA GLEESON. 2/6 ne (postage 3d.).

FATHERS OF THE DESERT, THE. By COUNTESS HAHN HAHN. Translated by EMILY F. BOWDEN, with a chapte on the Spiritual Life of the First Six Centuries by FATHE DALGAIRNS. 8s.

GERTRUDE, ST., LIFE AND REVELATIONS OF. By th Author of " St. Francis and the Franciscans." 7/6.

JOHN BAPTIST DE ROSSI, ST. Translated from th Italian by LADY HERBERT. A new edition, with a Introduction on Ecclesiastical Training and th Sacerdotal Life, by Cardinal Vaughan. 5/- net.

JOSEPH, LIFE AND GLORIES OF ST. By E. HEAL THOMPSON, M.A. 6/-.

KIRK'S BIOGRAPHIES OF THE ENGLISH CATHOLIC IN THE EIGHTEENTH CENTURY. Edited by FATHE POLLEN, S.J. 7/6 net.

LITTLE FLOWER OF JESUS, THE. The Autobiography c Sister Teresa, of the Child Jesus and the Holy Face Carmelite Nun. Three Portraits. 2/6 net (postage 4d.)

MELANIA, ST., LIFE OF. By H. E. CARDINAL RAMPOLLA Translated by E. LEAHY, and Edited by HERBER THURSTON, S.J. 4/6 net (postage 4d.).

MINIATURE LIVES OF THE SAINTS, for every Day in th Year. Edited by Rev. H. S. BOWDEN of the Oratory Two Vols. 4s.

MORE, LIFE AND WRITINGS OF BLESSED THOMAS By FATHER BRIDGETT, C.SS.R. 6/-.

MORE, LIFE OF BLESSED THOMAS. By his Son-in-law WILLIAM ROPER. With a Foreword by Mr. Justic Walton. 1/6 net (postage 2d.).

PATRICK, APOSTLE OF IRELAND, LIFE OF ST. B Rev. W. B. MORRIS. 2/6.

PHILIP NERI, LIFE OF ST. Translated from the Italia of CARDINAL CAPECELATRO by Rev. THOMAS ALDER POPE Two Vols. 12/6.

THOMAS AQUINAS, THE ANGELIC DOCTOR, LIFE OF ST. Edited by Rev. Pius Cavanagh, O.P. With eleven Illustrations. 4/6.

THOMAS OF AQUIN, THE LIFE AND LABOURS OF ST. By Archbishop Vaughan, O.S.B. Edited by Dom Jerome Vaughan, O.S.B. 6/6.

TWO LIVES OF OUR LORD FOR CHILDREN.

Jesus of Nazareth. By Mother M. Loyola. Illustrated. 5/- net (postage 4d.).

The Life of Our Lord, Written for Little Ones. By Mother M. Salome. 3/6.

WARD, MARY: A Foundress of the Seventeenth Century By Mother M. Salome, of the Bar Convent, York. With an Introduction by Bishop Hedley. Illustrated. 5s.

MISCELLANEOUS WORKS.

A BISHOP AND HIS FLOCK. By the Rt. Rev. John Cuthbert Hedley, O.S.B., Bishop of Newport. 6/-.

ALTAR SERVER'S MANUAL OF THE ARCHCONFRATERNITY OF ST. STEPHEN. Compiled by a Priest of the Archdiocese of Westminster. With an Introductory Preface by His Grace the Archbishop of Westminster. 1/- net (postage 2d.).

ANCIENT CATHOLIC HOMES OF SCOTLAND. By Dom Odo Blundell, O.S.B. With an Introduction by the Hon. Mrs. Maxwell Scott, of Abbotsford. Forty Illustrations. 3/6 net (postage 4d.).

CARMICHAEL, MONTGOMERY.

In Tuscany. New Edition, with numerous Illustrations. Large Cr. 8vo. 6s. net.

John William Walshe. The Story of a Hidden Life. 5/- net.

CHRIST, THE CHURCH, AND MAN, with some remarks on a New Apologia for Christianity in relation to the Social Question. By Cardinal Capecelatro, Archbishop of Capua. 2/- net (postage 3d.).

CHURCH AND KINDNESS TO ANIMALS, THE. Condemnation of Bull-fighting ; Animals in the Lives and Legends of Saints ; A Cloud of Witnesses. Illustrated. 2/6 net (postage 3d.).

ECCLESIA, THE CHURCH OF CHRIST. A Planned Series of Papers by Dom GILBERT DOLAN, O.S.B., FR. BENEDICT ZIMMERMANN, O.D.C., FATHER R. H. BENSON, M.A., DOM JOHN CHAPMAN, O.S.B., DOM J. D. BREEN, O.S.B., A. H. MATHEW, FATHER PETER FINLAY, S.J. Cloth, gilt, 3/6 net (postage 3d).

FOR MY NAME'S SAKE. From the French of CHAMPOL'S " Sœur Alexandrine." Illustrated by L. D. Symington. 3/6.

HOME FOR GOOD. By MOTHER M. LOYOLA. With Frontispiece. 3/6 net (postage 4d.)

LITTLE ANGELS, a Book of Comfort for Mourning Mothers. By FATHER MATTHEW RUSSELL, S.J. 2/6 net.

MAXIMS OF MADAME SWETCHINE, THE. Selected and Translated with a Biographical Note by I. A. TAYLOR. With a Portrait. Cloth, gilt, 2/- net (postage 2d.).

MODERN PILGRIM'S PROGRESS, A. 2nd Edition. With Introduction by the Very Rev. H. S. Bowden. 6/-.

NEW GUIDE TO THE HOLY LAND. With 23 Coloured Maps, and 110 Plans. By FR. BARNABAS MEISTERMANN, O.F.M. 7/6 net (postage 4d.).

ON RELIGIOUS WORSHIP, AND SOME DEFECTS IN POPULAR DEVOTION. A Pastoral Warning. By GEREMIA BONOMELLI, Bishop of Cremona. Together with a Letter to the English Translator, R. E. With the Author's Portrait. 2/6 net (postage 3d.).

REQUIESCANT. A Little Book of Anniversaries, arranged for daily use for those who love to remember the Faithful Departed. By MARY E. S. LEATHLEY. With an Introduction by Canon Murnane, V.G. 2/-.

SERVER'S MANUAL, THE. By JOHN LOUGHLIN. 1/- net.

SERVER'S MISSAL. A Practical Guide for Serving Boys at Mass. By a Sacristan. 6d.

Burns & Oates, 28 Orchard St., London, W.